CONTENTS

There are five important things you must know about your brain and memory to revolutionize the way you study:

◆ how your memory ("recall") works *while* you are learning
◆ how your memory works *after* you have finished learning
◆ how to use Mind Maps – a special technique for helping you with all aspects of your studies
◆ how to increase your reading speed
◆ how to prepare for tests and exams.

Recall during learning
– *THE NEED FOR BREAKS*

When you are studying, your memory can concentrate, understand, and remember well for between 20 and 45 minutes at a time, then it needs a break. If you continue for longer than this without a break your memory starts to break down. If you study for hours nonstop, you will remember only a small fraction of what you have been trying to learn, and you will have wasted hours of valuable time.

So, ideally, *study for less than an hour*, then take a five- to ten-minute break. During the break listen to music, go for a walk, do some exercise, or just daydream. (Daydreaming is a necessary brain-power booster – geniuses do it regularly.) During the break your brain will be sorting out what it has been learning, and you will go back to your books with the new information safely stored and organized in your memory. We recommend breaks at regular intervals as you work through the Literature Guides. Make sure you take them!

Recall after learning
– THE WAVES OF YOUR MEMORY

What do you think begins to happen to your memory right after you have finished learning something? Does it immediately start forgetting? No! Your brain actually *increases* its power and continues remembering. For a short time after your study session, your brain integrates the information, making a more complete picture of everything it has just learned. Only then does the rapid decline in memory begin, and as much as 80 percent of what you have learned can be forgotten in a day.

However, if you catch the top of the wave of your memory, and briefly review (look back over) what you have been studying at the correct time, the memory is imprinted far more strongly, and stays at the crest of the wave for a much longer time. To maximize your brain's power to remember, take a few minutes at the end of a day and use a Mind Map to review what you have learned. Then review it at the end of a week, again at the end of a month, and finally a week before your test or exam. That way you'll ride your memory wave all the way there – and beyond!

The Mind Map ®
– A PICTURE OF THE WAY YOU THINK

Do you like taking notes? More important, do you like having to go back over and learn them before tests or exams? Most students I know certainly do not! And how do you take your notes? Most people take notes on lined paper, using blue or black ink. The result, visually, is boring. And what does *your* brain do when it is bored? It turns off, tunes out, and goes to sleep! Add a dash of color, rhythm, imagination, and the whole note-taking process becomes much more fun, uses more of your brain's abilities, and improves your recall and understanding.

Generally, your Mind Map is highly personal and need not be understandable to any other person. It mirrors *your* brain. Its purpose is to build up your "memory muscle" by creating images that will help you recall instantly the most important points about characters and plot sequences in a work of fiction you are studying.

You will find Mind Maps throughout this book. Study them, add some color, personalize them, and then try drawing your own – you'll remember them far better. Stick them in your files and on your walls for a quick-and-easy review of the topic.

HOW TO DRAW A MIND MAP

1   First of all, briefly examine the Mind Maps and Mini Mind Maps used in this book. What are the common characteristics? All of them use small pictures or symbols, with words branching out from the illustration.

2   Decide which idea or character in the book you want to illustrate and then draw a picture, starting in the middle of the page so that you have plenty of room to branch out. Remember that no one expects a young Rembrandt or Picasso here; artistic ability is not as important as creating an image that you (and you alone) will remember. A round smiling (or sad) face might work as well in your memory as a finished portrait. Use marking pens of different colors to make your Mind Map as vivid and memorable as possible.

3   As your thoughts flow freely, add descriptive words and other ideas that connect to the central image. Print clearly, using one word per line if possible.

4   Further refine your thinking by adding smaller branching lines, containing less important facts and ideas, to connect with the main points.

5   Presto! You have a personal outline of your thoughts and concepts about the characters and the plot of the story. It's not a stodgy formal outline, but a colorful image that will stick in your mind, it is hoped, throughout classroom discussions and final exams.

HOW TO READ A MIND MAP

1   Begin in the center, the focus of your topic.

2   The words/images attached to the center are like chapter headings; read them next.

3   Always read out from the center, in every direction (even on the left-hand side, where you will have to read from right to left, instead of the usual left to right).

USING MIND MAPS

Mind Maps are a versatile tool; use them for taking notes in class or from books, for solving problems, for brainstorming with friends, and for reviewing and working for tests or exams – their uses are endless! You will find them invaluable for planning essays for coursework and exams. Number your main branches in the order in which you want to use them and off you go – the main headings for your essay are done and all your ideas are logically organized.

Preparing for tests and exams

◆ Review your work systematically. Cram at the beginning of your course, not the end, and avoid "exam panic!"
◆ Use Mind Maps throughout your course, and build a Master Mind Map for each subject – a giant Mind Map that summarizes everything you know about the subject.
◆ Use memory techniques such as mnemonics (verses or systems for remembering things like dates and events).
◆ Get together with one or two friends to study, compare Mind Maps, and discuss topics.

AND FINALLY...

Have *fun* while you learn – it has been shown that students who make their studies enjoyable understand and remember everything better and get the highest grades. I wish you and your brain every success! (Tony Buzan)

HOW TO USE THIS GUIDE

This guide assumes that you have already read *A Portrait of the Artist as a Young Man*, although you could read Background and The Story of *A Portrait of the Artist* before that. It is best to use the guide alongside the novel. You could read the Who's Who? and Themes sections without referring to the novel, but you will get more out of these sections if you refer to them to check the points made in these sections, especially when thinking about the questions designed to test your recall and help you think about the novel.

The different sections

The Commentary section can be used in a number of ways. One way is to read a chapter or part of a chapter in the novel, and then read the Commentary for that section. Continue until you come to a test section, test yourself, and then take a break. Or, read the Commentary for a chapter or part of a chapter, then read that section in the novel, then go back to the Commentary. Find out what works best for you.

Topics for Discussion and Brainstorming gives topics that could well appear on exams or provide a basis for coursework. It would be particularly useful for you to discuss them with friends, or brainstorm them using Mind Map techniques (see pp. vi and vii).

How to Get an "A" in English Literature gives valuable advice on what to look for in a text and what skills you need to develop in order to achieve your personal best.

The Exam Essay is a useful night-before reminder of how to tackle exam questions, and Model Answer and Essay Plan gives an example of an "A"-grade essay and the Mind Map and plan used to write it.

The questions

Whenever you come across a question in the guide with a star ✪ in front of it, think about it for a moment. You could even jot down a few words to focus your mind. There is not usually a "right" answer to the questions; it is important for you to develop your own opinions if you want to get an "A." The Test Yourself sections are designed to take you about 10–20 minutes each, which will be time well spent.

Key to icons

THEMES

A **theme** is an idea explored by an author. Whenever a theme is dealt with in the guide, the appropriate icon is used. This means you can find where a theme is mentioned just by flicking through the book. Try it now!

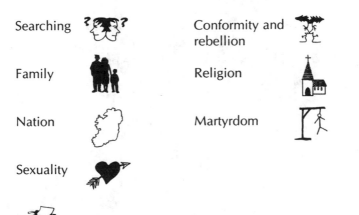

Searching		Conformity and rebellion	
Family		Religion	
Nation		Martyrdom	
Sexuality			

STYLE AND LANGUAGE

This heading and icon are used in the Commentary wherever you should pay special attention to the author's choice of words and **imagery** (a word picture used to make an idea come alive).

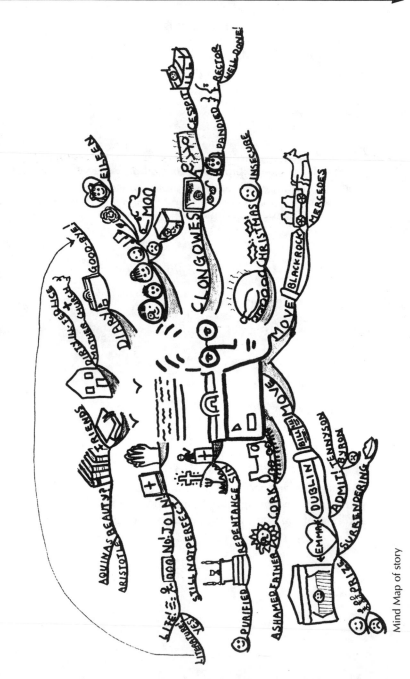

Mind Map of story

Is Stephen a portrait of James Joyce?

James Joyce was born in Dublin on February 2, 1882, the eldest of ten surviving children. (Several others died.) His family lived in the places mentioned in the novel. Joyce was sent to Clongowes Wood College but left after three years because his father was not able to cope with his money problems.

The family became poverty-stricken soon after moving into the center of Dublin. Joyce was given a free place at the Jesuit day school, Belvedere, where he remained as a student until he entered University College in 1898. He received his degree in 1902 and almost immediately left for Paris.

The following year his mother's illness brought Joyce back to Ireland. In late 1904, after her death, he returned to Europe. He took with him Norah Barnacle, the "Rosie O'Grady" whom Stephen still has not met by the end of *A Portrait*. Joyce's later visits to Ireland were always brief; he spent the rest of his life teaching and writing in Italy, Switzerland, and France.

This outline suggests that *A Portrait* follows Joyce's years of growing up very closely. If you look at a detailed biography of the writer, you will find an even greater resemblance between his own background and Stephen's.

All Joyce's fiction was created out of his early life in Ireland. *A Portrait* contains far more autobiographical detail than *Jane Eyre* by Charlotte Brontë or *David Copperfield* by Charles Dickens, both of which are partly autobiographical.

AUTOBIOGRAPHICAL FICTION

Autobiographical fiction usually follows the main character from childhood to whatever point the author has decided to make the end of the story. The hero/heroine is involved with different characters at different stages of life and remains the dominant point of interest. The story tells of struggle against misfortune and hostility. Most frequently the novel has an "I" narrator.

In stories of this kind an adult passes on thoughts about his or her childhood to the reader. The writer-narrator may frankly admit weaknesses and bad behavior, and the other characters may be more than black-and-white; still, the *writer's* aim is to make us identify with the main character, be indignant at what he or she suffers, and always take his or her side against the other characters. The narrative contains very clear signposts to bring out these reactions in us, for example, the way Jane Eyre is treated at Lowood.

✪ Can you think of other examples from autobiographical novels you may have read?

Despite its parallels with Joyce's own life *A Portrait* does not conform to the above description. The autobiographical content is not there to reveal the author's life, to make the story realistic by using his own experience, or to get back at old enemies and justify his actions to people who have criticized them. One or more of these motives usually prompts the writing of autobiographical fiction.

A UNIVERSAL TRUTH

Joyce has an entirely different purpose here, which is summed up in the title. If you are reading this section as part of your review, try to describe for yourself what it is before going on. Rereading Chapter 5 will help. (Throughout the book, *art*, *artist*, *artistic*, and so on, refer to literature, not the visual arts, which might be our first associations with these words today.)

Joyce draws on his own history to examine the way in which a great artist's talent first reveals itself and then develops through childhood and adolescence. The novel tries to present a universal truth, a portrait of the artist in general or as a type, not the portrait of any individual artist, such as Joyce himself. This is why we are not given a full picture of Stephen's early years. Joyce uses only incidents that are relevant to his purpose. Anything else is left out or mentioned very briefly.

Moreover, despite the close resemblance to the author's own background, there are major differences between the young Joyce – a cheerful extrovert who was popular with his fellow students – and Stephen Dedalus. The hero of *A Portrait* has no such defenses against the pressures of the outside world. By intensifying the conflict between Stephen and his environment, and paring down the narrative, Joyce reinforces the intended effect of his novel.

This relationship between a general truth and the particular details that embody it is an important part of your study of this novel. If you find the idea too hard to grasp at present, make another attempt when studying the theory of art and beauty that Stephen puts forward in Chapter 5.

A *new kind of novel*

Up to the beginning of the twentieth century, almost all novelists told a story by dividing their material between dialogue, description, straightforward narration, and thoughts supposed to be passing through the characters' minds. Authors were judged on their skill at blending and balancing these elements so as to provide "a good read."

Within this framework the story might proceed in a straight line or contain flashbacks in time. It might be told by a central "I" figure or from the viewpoint of one or more of the characters. Whichever method was used, readers were always aware of the author in the background, acting as a kind of tour guide to the world into which they were invited.

The author's presence was a particular feature of Victorian fiction. "Reader, I married him!" cries Charlotte Brontë's heroine when she finally falls into the arms of Mr. Rochester.

Toward the end of the nineteenth century, writers began to look for different ways of representing experience. There was much research at the time on the workings of the unconscious mind, and this led to the realization that the traditional style of novel writing was only one possibility. If they wished, writers could get much closer to the real thoughts, feelings, and actions that go on throughout the day for each one of us.

Try this experiment. Write down a sentence something like this: *I got up from my chair, walked to the window, and looked out to see if the cat was in the garden.* Then try to do exactly that and nothing else. You will find it impossible. As you leave your chair you will catch sight of an object that

3

makes you think of something else; on your way to the window the same thing will happen; when you look out of the window, if you do see the cat, you will also catch sight of, say, an old piece of paper blowing along the pavement and think about that. And so on.

STREAM OF CONSCIOUSNESS

The writer who tries to catch this full flow of perception is using a technique known as **stream of consciousness**. Joyce's later and most famous novel, *Ulysses*, in which Stephen Dedalus reappears, is written using this technique. The method is not fully developed in *A Portrait*, although the novel is moving toward it when Stephen is bracing himself to confront the rector. *He was walking down along the matting and he saw the door before him. It was impossible: he could not.* Here, without warning, we pass directly from what Stephen sees to what Stephen thinks.

Stream of consciousness and other new techniques developed by writers such as James Joyce have affected all modern fiction to some degree, even though the majority of novels still follow the traditional pattern.

Under the influence of earlier writers, such as the French novelist Flaubert, Joyce tried to remove the author's voice altogether. In *A Portrait* much of the usual "padding" disappears and, as mentioned earlier, the action is restricted to key episodes in the hero's life. Everything is seen through the consciousness of Stephen Dedalus. There are no transition passages between one episode and the next, and dialogue, narrative, and interior monologue frequently merge into each other.

The story is told in straightforward chronological order, but the separate episodes are connected in an intricate pattern of symbolism and imagery of a kind more often found in **lyric verse**. The language is brilliantly versatile, ranging from the most down-to-earth realism to passages containing so many images and intricate word rhythms that we may call them **prose poetry**. Joyce also shows great skill in keeping his hero, Stephen, in "double focus," with the result that that we both identify with him and stand apart.

James Joyce and Ireland

For most people on the British mainland, "Ireland" means the ongoing problems of the two warring sides in Northern Ireland. Today, this is part of the United Kingdom and quite distinct from the independent Republic of Ireland to the south of it.

The situation was entirely different when Joyce wrote *A Portrait*. There is no need to study the background in great detail, but you must know enough to understand why politics play such an important part in the book.

At the time in which the story is set, the whole island of Ireland was ruled by the British government in London. It had been occupied by English – later British – troops and settlers since the Middle Ages. The dominant cultural forces were the Anglican Church of Ireland and Anglo-Irish landowners. The latter considered themselves Irish but, in fact, they were part of the ruling class of Great Britain, even though some of them supported the campaign for Irish Home Rule. The social and political attitudes produced by this situation are accurately reflected in *A Portrait*.

Agitation for Home Rule had begun in the early 1800s, soon after the Irish Parliament was abolished. The difficulties caused by Irish nationalism and British reluctance to let go were aggravated by the terrible Irish potato famine of the 1840s.

Later in the nineteenth century, a number of the cultural movements mentioned in *A Portrait* were started up to encourage the Irish to be proud of their native traditions. There were also a few secret underground societies, but no effective rebellion until well into the twentieth century.

In 1920 the Government of Ireland Act led to the establishing of the Irish Free State, now known as the Republic of Ireland. At the same time, six of the nine counties of Ulster – those with a Protestant majority – voted to remain within the United Kingdom. The results of this division actively influence the politics of Ireland today.

THE STORY OF *A PORTRAIT OF THE ARTIST*

Look at the story Mind Map on p. x while reading this.

Stephen Dedalus is the eldest child of a Catholic family living in **Bray**, a seaside resort about 18 miles south of Dublin. The time is the late nineteenth century. The family consists of Stephen's father, who is a minor **civil servant**, his mother, his father's Uncle Charles, and Mrs. Riordan – "**Dante**" – who acts as nurse to Stephen and the large number of brothers and sisters born after him. Stephen is a **sensitive**, perceptive child who is fascinated by **words** from an early age. He has poor eyesight but, as if to make up for this, his other senses are highly developed.

When the story opens, the family is relatively prosperous, although Mr. Dedalus's inability to **manage his financial affairs** is soon to reduce them to poverty. He is determined to give his son a good education – mostly for snobbish reasons, it seems – and at the age of six Stephen is sent to **Clongowes Wood College**, a prestigious boys' boarding school run by the **Jesuits**.

Stephen is a willing, obedient pupil, but he finds it hard to settle into his new environment. He is no good at **sports** and cannot stand up for himself when he is **bullied**. An older boy pushes him into a cesspool, and he comes down with a fever. Stephen has to spend some time in the school **infirmary**.

The longed-for Christmas vacation turns into a disaster when Mrs. Riordan has a violent **quarrel** with Stephen's father and his guest over the Christmas dinner. They disagree about **Parnell**, the Irish Home Rule leader denounced by the Church for his adulterous relationship with the wife of a fellow **politician**. Mrs. Riordan supports the **priests**; the others take the side of Parnell. Stephen is bewildered by the squabbling and raised voices of the adults, and the sight of his father **weeping** over the death of Parnell terrifies him.

On his return to **Clongowes**, Stephen manages to fit in better with the school and its ways although he is perplexed by behavior he is too young to understand. After being **caned** unfairly by the sadistic prefect of studies, he complains to the **rector**, who promises to set matters right. This incident wins Stephen acceptance by the other students, who regard him as a **hero**.

Mr. Dedalus's loss of **income** makes it impossible for Stephen to continue to attend Clongowes. The family moves to **Blackrock**, a suburb south of Dublin. Stephen becomes an avid **reader** and begins to live in a fantasy world to compensate for the growing poverty of everyday life. As he moves into **adolescence**, he searches restlessly for some outlet for his awakening **sexuality**.

The family is forced to move into **Dublin** itself, where Stephen reluctantly accompanies his mother on visits to her relatives. He becomes interested in a girl named **Emma Clery**, but is too timid to press his attentions on her. Mr. Dedalus meets the rector of Clongowes and secures from him a free place for **Stephen** and his brother, **Maurice**, at **Belvedere**, the Jesuits' day school in Dublin.

Stephen is successful at **Belvedere**. He wins respect as one of its best students and becomes the **prefect** of the religious brotherhood of Mary, but he is becoming increasingly **restless** and **moody**. He rebels against the values of his companions and is **tormented** by his unsatisfied sexual urges.

Mr. Dedalus returns to his native Cork to sell off some **property** and takes Stephen with him. Stephen is deeply **ashamed** of his father's behavior. Mr. Dedalus parades around his old haunts, **drinking** and boasting and indulging in sentimental memories.

Stephen tries to restore his family's **respectability** by buying them small treats and luxuries out of the money he has won in an **essay** competition. This has no effect in the long run; Mr. Dedalus has dragged his family into a descending spiral of **poverty**. They move from one **address** to another as they find themselves unable to pay the **rent**. Goaded on *by the wasting fires of lust*, Stephen begins to prowl around the streets of Dublin by night. One evening he makes his way to an area of **brothels**, where a **prostitute** at last satisfies his sexual need.

Visiting this part of the city becomes a regular habit for Stephen until the rector of Belvedere announces a **retreat** in honor of

St. Francis Xavier. Stephen is subjected to several days of hellfire **sermons** about the ultimate fate of the wicked and, as a result, is overwhelmed with **fear** and **remorse** for his indulgence in sexual acts. He imposes on himself a series of **penances** that take up most of his waking time.

The director of Belvedere interviews **Stephen** to find out if he has a vocation for the **priesthood**. By now, Stephen's respect for his **tutors** has been undermined, yet he is highly responsive to church ritual. He is tempted by the power and status that the **priesthood** would bring him. Once he leaves the **director's** study, Stephen realizes that he does not want to commit himself to the restricted, **communal** life of a Jesuit. He prefers to be involved in the disorder of everyday life with all its **imperfections**.

Stephen still does not know what the purpose of his life is to be, but he has decided to enroll in the **university**. While he awaits the outcome of his father's meeting with a university tutor, he walks beside the **sea** and receives an ecstatic vision that reveals his vocation to be an **artist**.

As a **student**, Stephen gathers around him a group of **companions** whose interests he shares only fitfully. He realizes more and more that he must detach himself from the claims of **home**, **country**, and **religion** if he is to fulfill his destiny and not sink into the self-oppressing culture – as he perceives it – of those around him.

During this time Stephen sketches out a theory of **aesthetics** that points to the ideal standards he will aspire to in his own art. His break with the **Church** leads to a serious dispute with his mother. **Cranly**, Stephen's closest friend at the **university** advises him to perform his "Easter duty," in other words, go to **mass** and take Communion, if only to spare his mother's feelings.

Stephen has decided that to be himself he will have to leave **Ireland** altogether. The last part of the story deals with his efforts to confirm his decision by breaking the ties that bind him to **country**, **home**, and **religion**. He manages to cast off even the obsession with **Emma** that has dogged him for ten years. Stephen's last act in the novel is to invoke the spirit of his namesake, **Daedalus**, the cunning craftsman, and ask him to aid him in his flight.

HOW MUCH CAN YOU REMEMBER?

Try to fill in the missing words from this summary without looking back at the original text. Feel free to use your own words if they have the same meaning.

Stephen Dedalus is the eldest child of a Catholic family living in _____ , a seaside resort about 18 miles south of Dublin. The time is the late nineteenth century. The family consists of Stephen's father, who is a minor _____ _____, his mother, his father's Uncle Charles, and Mrs. Riordan – "_____ " – who acts as nurse to Stephen and the large number of brothers and sisters born after him. Stephen is a _____ , perceptive child who is fascinated by _____ from an early age. He has poor eyesight but, as if to make up for this, his other senses are highly developed.

When the story opens, the family is relatively prosperous, although Mr. Dedalus's inability to _____ _____ _____ _____ is soon to drive them into poverty. He is determined to give his son a good education – mostly for snobbish reasons, it seems – and at the age of six Stephen is sent to _____ _____ _____ , a prestigious boys' boarding school run by the _____.

Stephen is a willing, obedient pupil, but he finds it hard to settle into his new environment. He is no good at _____ and cannot stand up for himself when he is ____. An older boy pushes him into a cesspool and he comes down with a fever. Stephen has to spend some time in the school _____ .

The longed-for Christmas vacation turns into a disaster when Mrs. Riordan has a violent _____ with Stephen's father and his guest over the Christmas dinner. They disagree about _____, the Irish Home Rule leader denounced by the Church for his adulterous relationship with the wife of a fellow _____. Mrs. Riordan supports the _____; the others take the side of Parnell. Stephen is bewildered by the squabbling and raised voices of the adults, and the sight of his father _____ over the death of Parnell terrifies him.

On his return to _____ Stephen manages to fit in better with the school and its ways although he is perplexed by behavior he is too young to understand. After being _____ unfairly by

9

the sadistic prefect of studies he complains to the _____, who promises to set matters right. This incident wins Stephen acceptance by the other students, who regard him as a _____.

Mr. Dedalus's loss of _____ makes it impossible for Stephen to continue to attend Clongowes. The family moves to _____, a suburb south of Dublin. Stephen becomes an avid _____ and begins to live in a fantasy world to compensate for the growing poverty of everyday life. As he moves into _____, he searches restlessly for some outlet for his awakening _____.

The family is forced to move into _____ itself, where Stephen reluctantly accompanies his mother on visits to her relatives. He becomes interested in a girl named _____ _____ but is too timid to press his attentions on her. Mr. Dedalus meets the rector of Clongowes and secures from him a free place for _____ and his brother _____ at _____, the Jesuits' day school in Dublin.

Stephen is successful at _____. He wins respect as one of its best students and becomes the _____ of the religious brotherhood of Mary, but he is becoming increasingly _____ and _____. He rebels against the values of his companions and is _____ by his unsatisfied sexual urges.

Mr. Dedalus returns to his native Cork to sell off some _____ and takes Stephen with him. Stephen is deeply _____ of his father's behavior. Mr. Dedalus parades around his old haunts, _____ and boasting and indulging in sentimental memories.

Stephen tries to restore his family's _____ by buying them small treats and luxuries out of the money he has won in an _____ competition. This has no effect in the long run; Mr. Dedalus has dragged his family into a descending spiral of _____. They move from one _____ to another as they find themselves unable to pay the _____. Goaded on *by the wasting fires of lust,* Stephen begins to prowl around the streets of Dublin by night. One evening he makes his way to an area of _____, where a _____ at last satisfies his sexual need.

Visiting this part of the city becomes a regular habit for Stephen until the rector of Belvedere announces a _____ in honor of St. Francis Xavier. Stephen is subjected to several days of hellfire _____ about the ultimate fate of the wicked and, as a result, is overwhelmed with _____ and _____ for his indulgence in sexual acts. He imposes on himself a series of _____ that take up most of his waking time.

The director of Belvedere interviews _____ to find out if he has a vocation for the _____. By now Stephen's respect for his _____ has been undermined, yet he is highly responsive to church ritual. He is tempted by the power and status that the _____ would bring him. Once he leaves the _____ study, Stephen realizes that he does not want to commit himself to the restricted, _____ life of a Jesuit. He prefers to be involved in the disorder of everyday life with all its

_____.

Stephen still does not know what the purpose of his life is to be, but he has decided to enroll in the _____. While he awaits the outcome of his father's meeting with a university tutor, he walks beside the _____ and receives an ecstatic vision that reveals his vocation to be an _____.

As a _____, Stephen gathers around him a group of _____ whose interests he shares only fitfully. He realizes more and more that he must detach himself from the claims of _____, _____, and _____ if he is to fulfill his destiny and not sink into the self-oppressing culture – as he perceives it – of those around him.

During this time Stephen sketches out a theory of _____ that points to the ideal standards he will aspire to in his own art. His break with the _____ leads to a serious dispute with his mother. _____, Stephen's closest friend at _____ advises him to perform his "Easter duty," in other words, go to _____ and take Communion, if only to spare his mother's feelings.

Stephen has decided that to be himself he will have to leave _____ altogether. The last part of the story deals with his efforts to confirm his decision by breaking the ties that bind him to _____, _____, and _____. He manages to cast off even the obsession with _____ that has dogged him for ten years. Stephen's last act in the novel is to invoke the spirit of his namesake, _____, the cunning craftsman, and ask him to aid him in his flight.

WHO'S WHO?

The Mini Mind Map above summarizes the character groups in *A Portrait*. Test yourself by looking at the full Mind Map on p. 20 and then copying the Mini Mind Map and trying to add to it from memory.

A Portrait has a fairly straightforward time structure, and characters fit into obvious groups. The novel inevitably has a large cast, but only the most important characters will be discussed here. We will look at Stephen at the end.

Group 1 – the Dedalus family

SIMON DEDALUS

Simon Dedalus is a family man with strong affections but no sense of responsibility. He delights in playing the generous host to friends and dependants at the Dedalus Christmas dinner, but cannot resist egging John Casey on to tell a story that provokes a major row with Mrs. Riordan. ✪ Why does he do this? Could it have anything to do with his attitude toward her? Do they like each other? Look closely at the way they speak to each other before the quarrel begins.

Mr. Dedalus's attitude toward life is outgoing and optimistic. Even when faced with financial disaster, he does not stay depressed for long. The visit to Cork has a serious purpose – to raise some desperately needed money – but Mr. Dedalus spends most of his time there flirting, boasting, and drinking. ✪ Is this a brave attempt to hide his worries from Stephen, or is he running away from reality?

One of the more comic passages in *A Portrait* is the description of Simon Dedalus assuring his embarrassed son as he drags him around the haunts of his youth, *I'm talking to you as a friend, Stephen, I don't believe in playing the stern father.*

Mr. Dedalus is a fluent, racy talker, full of anecdotes and clever imitations, and no doubt an amusing companion in the pub. He is also vain, complacent, and snobbish – the last a trait he has passed on to his eldest son. He wants to give Stephen a good education to make sure he will mix with *gentlemen ... and bloody good honest Irishmen*, and thus keep up the family's social status.

It is hard to tell whether Mr. Dedalus's enthusiasm for Parnell springs from genuine conviction or is just part of his sentimental, excitable nature. ✪ What do you think? We might say the same about the contempt he shows for Church and clergy at the Christmas dinner table. These opinions are conveniently forgotten when he wants to send Stephen to a school run by the Jesuits. He makes a great show of being a rebel – perhaps to goad Dante – but in practice he accepts his country's institutions as unquestioningly as anyone.

While quite unable to assess what other people really think of him, Simon Dedalus places great value on personal contacts. This is clearly shown in his meetings with his old Cork acquaintances. ✪ Can you think of other examples in the book?

Stephen's description of his father—*A medical student, an oarsman, a tenor, an amateur actor, a shouting politician, ... a drinker, a good fellow, ... and at present a praiser of his own past*—completes the picture of a man of many talents betrayed by his own lack of willpower. In his last appearance in the story, probably suffering from a hangover after another drinking bout, he shouts downstairs, *Is your lazy bitch of a brother gone out yet?*

MARY DEDALUS

Mary Dedalus is a devout Catholic and a loyal, submissive wife. She has had nine or ten children of whom *some died.*   **13**

Cranly remarks to Stephen, *Your mother must have gone through a good deal of suffering*, but by that time Stephen takes her very much for granted.

At their Christmas dinner, Mrs. Dedalus pleads for *no political discussion on this day of all days in the year*. Her reprimands are too gentle to halt the quarrel, showing that she has no strong influence on her husband's behavior then or later.

She is more outspoken with her eldest son, telling him *it's a poor case* that she still has to wash him and that the university has changed him for the worse. Her *listless silence* when Stephen first goes there shows she was opposed to the idea from the beginning. ✪ Are you surprised at this, when she supported her husband in sending Stephen to "good" schools? Look at what the director of Belvedere says about the priesthood (the sentence beginning *To receive that call, Stephen ...*). ✪ Is Mrs. Dedalus likely to share this opinion? How might that affect her attitude when Stephen turned down the opportunity offered him by the director?

We may be sure that Mary Dedalus will suffer far more over the quarrel with her son than Stephen will. As he prepares to leave Ireland, one of Stephen's diary entries reveals that his mother understands him better than he understands himself. *She prays now, she says, that I may learn in my own life and away from home and friends what the heart is and what it feels.* ✪ What does Mrs. Dedalus mean?

DANTE

Mrs. Riordan ("Dante") appears only in the first chapter. Her function is to act as nurse and governess to the younger children, and she seems to have joined the household soon after Stephen was born. Presumably she left after the violent Christmas quarrel. In any case, within a few years the family would be too poor to continue to employ her. Apparently she is not with them in Blackrock or Dublin.

Dante is *a clever woman and a wellread woman* who once intended to become a nun. She is fiercely anti-Protestant, trying to break up Stephen's friendship with Eileen Vance because of their difference in religion. Judging by Stephen's early memories, she was strict in carrying out her duties.

Dante has an assertive personality. The only characteristic she shares with Mrs. Dedalus is an unquestioning respect for the Church. She cannot hold her tongue when Mr. Dedalus and his friend, John Casey, criticize the priests for their part in Parnell's downfall. ✪ Do you think they set about provoking her deliberately?

UNCLE CHARLES

Uncle Charles (Mr. Dedalus's uncle), *a hale old man with a welltanned skin, rugged features and white side whiskers,* is a comfortable background figure in the family. At the Christmas dinner he adds his remarks to those of Mary Dedalus, trying to stifle the developing quarrel, with the same result. After the move to Blackrock we see him fitting placidly into a domestic routine. He helps out with the shopping and accompanies Mr. Dedalus and Stephen on ten-mile Sunday walks. Stephen respects his piety. Like all the Dedalus family, Uncle Charles enjoys singing. His only act of rebellion is to smoke foul-smelling tobacco, for which he is banished to an outhouse at the end of the garden.

Stephen's brother and sisters make minimal appearances in the book. (This is an excellent example of the way Joyce omits details not relevant to his purpose. We would normally expect to learn much more about the brothers and sisters with whom our hero grows up.) Although Maurice accompanies Stephen to Belvedere, that is all we learn about him. The three sisters are not identified or named until late in the book.

Group 2 – Clongowes Wood College

In his early days as a student here, Stephen finds most of the "fellows" hostile and threatening. Later, he makes some friendships, but none of them seems to outlast his leaving the school. A far greater impact is made on him by the **prefects**, or masters, who are all Jesuit priests.

FATHER ARNALL

Father Arnall makes two appearances. His first is as a Latin teacher to Stephen's junior class at Clongowes. Several years later he comes to Dublin to deliver the retreat sermons to the schoolboys at Belvedere.

In the Latin lesson he is enraged because the "themes" – homework exercises – have been done so badly. He lets his anger show, but in a controlled manner. After the pandying (caning) episode when both Stephen and his friend Fleming are beaten by Father Dolan, Father Arnall goes around the class *helping the boys with gentle words and telling them the mistakes they had made. His voice was very gentle and soft.*

❂ What does this change of attitude tell us about Father Arnall? Is he trying to make up for Father Dolan's harshness? Or is he feeling less angry because he has had the satisfaction of seeing two boys punished? He tells the other priest that Stephen has broken his glasses, but he doesn't try to stop the unfair punishment. Why not?

The retreat sermons are full of frightening, gory images and Father Arnall never does get around to describing the joys of heaven. ❂ Allowing for the fact that he is preaching orthodox Catholic doctrine, what does this later appearance tell us about Father Arnall's character?

FATHER DOLAN

Father Dolan is the prefect of studies at Clongowes; he supervises the courses that each boy takes. ❂ What would you expect to find in his job description? What does he seem to think his duties are? When he enters the room there is *a quick whisper* and *an instant of dead silence*. What does this tell us about his reputation among the boys?

Father Dolan has a *whitegrey not young face ... baldy whitegrey head* and *noncoloured eyes*. As well as beating the pupils with sadistic relish, he torments them psychologically, forcing them to repeat his words.

He is the most frightening of the authority figures at Clongowes. However, since the other masters excuse his behavior – as Stephen finds out – we may say that they are all tainted with his cruelty.

Group 3 – Belvedere

A great many new characters enter the story when the Dedalus family moves into Dublin. Stephen comes into contact with several of his mother's relatives; his attendance at Belvedere, the Jesuits' day school, places him among a fresh group of schoolboys.

Vincent Heron is the only one who stands out. He has *a high throaty voice* and *a ... mobile face, beaked like a bird's.* He is a bit of a poser (phony), carries a cane, and makes a great show of being sophisticated. When Stephen first enrolls at Belvedere, Heron and two other boys bully him severely, but at the time of the Whitsuntide play, Stephen and Heron are regarded as joint heads of the school.

Group 4 – University College, Dublin

In the long final chapter, several of Stephen's fellow students are presented in detail.

CRANLY

Cranly is a complex character with depths that are only hinted at. He has *stiff black upright hair ... a priestlike face, ... widewinged nose ... lips ...long and bloodless and faintly smiling.* He skips lectures to go to the races.

Cranly's feelings are tightly repressed. ● Is this what lies behind his air of *listlessness* and the outbursts of irritation with Temple and Goggins? He hears Stephen's confidences sometimes in *listening silence* and sometimes with *harsh comments* and *sudden intrusions of rude speech*.

Stephen uses Cranly to sort out his own feelings about the quarrel with his mother. Their conversation reveals that Cranly believes in the Church and its doctrines, though in a more relaxed way than "Dante" or Mrs. Dedalus. He has an intuitive understanding of other people. Although he lacks Stephen's courage, his awareness of Mary Dedalus's situation shows that he is more emotionally mature than his friend.

DAVIN

Davin is a frank, unself-conscious *peasant student* with a *rude Firbolg mind* who calls Stephen "Stevie." He is an athlete and fierce Irish nationalist, hating everything associated with the British occupation of his country. He has been brought up on Irish myth and legend and sees national problems in the same heroic terms. In Stephen's opinion his attitude toward both Ireland and the Roman Catholic religion is that of *a dullwitted loyal serf.*

Davin tells Stephen about an encounter he had with a countrywoman when he was walking home from a hurling (a type of hockey) match outside Dublin. She was alone and invited him in for the night, but Davin refused. ❂ What does this tell us about him? He is shocked and upset when Stephen confides the details of his "private life" – presumably his visits to prostitutes.

Lynch, **MacCann**, and **Temple** also appear in several parts of the last chapter. They figure as distinct characters but do not interact so closely with Stephen as Cranly and Davin. They are there to typify aspects of Irish life and society. ❂ Can you suggest what these might be?

EMMA CLERY

Emma Clery – *the temptress of his villanelle* – is the object of Stephen's sexual feelings for a large part of the book. She is attracted to him; when he does not respond she remains friendly but does not renew the invitation. This is perfectly natural behavior, although Stephen does not see it like that.

Stephen's inability to understand the situation leads to his construction of a fantasy figure that bears no resemblance to Emma as a real, live, young woman. Joyce's skill lies in making this obvious without going into much detail about her character and appearance. After all, it is the fantasy Emma who is important to this picture of the hero's development.

❂ Make a Mind Map of the real-life encounters between Stephen and Emma and discuss how they might have been interpreted by Emma. Support your opinions with details from the text.

Stephen

Stephen is not only the main character in *A Portrait*; his mental processes, consciousness, and way of perceiving the world are its main subject. You should try to show you know this if you answer a question that involves assessing Stephen in the same way as the other characters in the book: a description of their appearance, the characteristics that make them behave in the way they do, their importance to the story, and their relationship to other figures in the book.

Joyce stresses only the aspects of Stephen's character that are relevant to the themes of the book and leaves others unexplored. Likewise, what happens to him is restricted to key episodes only, and we have to work out the rest from Stephen's reactions or remarks made by other characters.

These aspects are covered in detail in the Commentary. Stephen's most obvious characteristic is his acute **sensitivity**, physical as well as emotional. Every new sensation affects him intensely, and he reacts badly to the pressures of growing up.

By nature, Stephen wants to **conform**, but he is too intelligent to miss the imperfections in people and institutions around him. Where others might compromise, he is unable to come to terms with his disillusionment. The resulting tension creates an introspective personality, acutely aware of its own loneliness and isolation.

Stephen's **courage** is another well-illustrated feature – his interview with the rector at Clongowes, his championship of Byron against Tennyson at Belvedere, and his determination to strike out for himself, intellectually and artistically, at University College. It is this aspect of his character that enables him finally to face up to the choices he must make to fulfill his vocation.

Another important character trait is **egotism**, that is, Stephen's complete self-absorption in Stephen. This results in a passive personality, someone who fits in with what is going on around him because he has no direct emotional connection with other people. Toward the end of the book, Stephen is beginning to rebel openly; he tries to explain his ideas and feelings to fellow students. ✪ Do you think this means that he is becoming more aware of other people, or will egotism always be a permanent feature of Stephen's character?

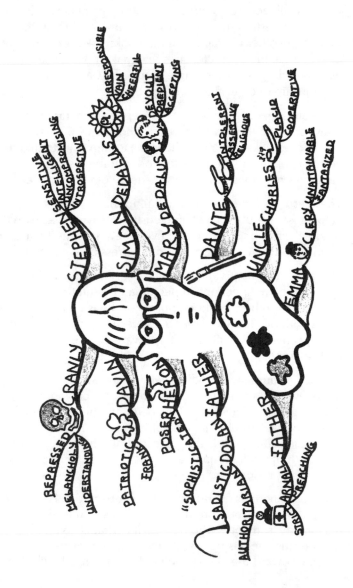

Themes

A **theme** is an idea developed or explored throughout a work (a play, book, poem, and so on). The main themes of *A Portrait* are shown in the Mini Mind Map above and can be identified as follows:

- searching
- conformity and rebellion
- family
- religion
- nation
- martyrdom
- sexuality

Test yourself on the themes by copying the Mini Mind Map above, adding to it yourself, and then comparing your results with the full Mind Map on p. 27.

Joyce himself said that the main theme of *A Portrait* was "the renegade Catholic artist as hero." This is several steps into the actual contents of the novel. To discover its "meaning" – the general ideas that lie behind Joyce's use of his material – we need to ask ourselves, what kind of hero is Stephen?

Searching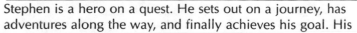

Stephen is a hero on a quest. He sets out on a journey, has adventures along the way, and finally achieves his goal. His

21

quest is not for treasure or the Holy Grail or a sleeping princess. He searches for understanding and self-knowledge.

From his first conscious moments, Stephen is trying to make sense of the world around him. He ponders deeply about each sense impression as it presents itself, and his curiosity about the meaning of words is strikingly intense.

It is this very inquisitiveness – and his poor eyesight – that promote the development of Stephen's inward-looking personality. From an early age he is so involved with the excitements of his own mind that he cuts himself off from a lot of the normal comradeship of boyhood.

As he grows up, his sense of being different and apart from other people – his "alienation" – drives Stephen deeper and deeper into his own imagination. Exploring his own thought processes becomes an end in itself as well as a refuge. "He lives in a world of his own," to use a cliché. He begins to return to the real world when he discovers his vocation as an artist.

Conformity and rebellion

The conflict between conformity and rebellion is another important theme. As a young child Stephen is anxious to conform and do what he is told. Right up to the end of his school days he keeps his *habits of quiet obedience*. He does not voice his rebellious thoughts until he is a student.

In fact, it is this inability to discuss and communicate that gives rise to a lot of Stephen's problems. He needs to find out for himself without consulting others. His quest for knowledge inevitably leads him to notice contradictions in adult behavior, and he feels betrayed. After the horrors of his first term at Clongowes, he looks forward to vacation, but his homecoming exposes him to a violent quarrel over the family Christmas dinner.

Through being caned unjustly, he also discovers that his teachers do not live up to the high standards they expect of their students. Through one disillusionment after another, he is driven to reject the values with which he has grown up. He does not give them up lightly; the process is long and painful.

Family, religion, and nation

Finally Stephen finds himself in revolt against his family, his religion, and his nation. (Each of these has an icon that you will find linked with that of the main theme at various points in the Commentary.) When his belief systems collapse around him, Stephen cannot take a detached view, as Cranly suggests. The pressures of being an outsider are intolerable, and he has to escape if he is to fulfill his vocation as an artist.

Joyce also develops the theme of conformity and rebellion by frequently reminding us of associations attached to the names "Stephen" and "Dedalus." Dedalus is slightly altered from the name of the Athenian craftsman who was imprisoned by King Minos, but escaped with his son Icarus by constructing wings from bird feathers, held together by wax. The whole novel is saturated with references to this Greek myth. Flight imagery – in both senses of the word – occurs throughout the novel, while Stephen's attempts to escape from his own labyrinth are symbolized by walks and night wanderings. These, in turn, can be linked with the first theme, the hero's search for understanding and self-knowledge. In the Greek myth, young Icarus soars too high, the sun melts his waxen wings, and he drowns in the sea.

Martyrdom

Stephen, the first Christian martyr, was denounced to the Jewish council as a blasphemer and stoned to death. When Stephen Dedalus refuses to conform, he too is persecuted (as when he claims that Byron is a better poet than Tennyson). However, as we would expect from Joyce, the comparison is not always so obvious. A martyr is not just someone who suffers, but someone who could choose not to suffer by renouncing some cause or dearly held belief. ✪ Can you think of any other incidents when Stephen is "martyred" in this sense? This subtheme of martyrdom can be seen also in the passages about Parnell and the Countess Cathleen, and even in the references to Cranly as the "precursor."

Sexuality

Stephen suffers an extreme form of adolescent difficulty with sexuality. We could argue that this is part of his alienation from others, but it plays such an important role in the book that it deserves a separate examination.

Apart from his father, most of the adult males that Stephen comes into contact with are celibate Roman Catholic priests who impose a rigidly disciplined and authoritarian viewpoint on the children in their care. As a schoolboy both at Clongowes and in Dublin, Stephen spends most of his day in an all-male environment. At home his mother and sisters exist to serve the favored eldest son. Even when he goes to the university with its quota of woman students, Stephen continues to spend most of his time with other young men.

All this was normal at a time when young people were not allowed to mix as freely as they do today. Look at the conversation of Stephen's friends at school and the university. ○ What evidence can you find that the conditions described above did not have the same effect on them? Why not?

In Stephen's case a strong guilt feeling toward women is implanted at an early age. His affection for Eileen Vance is brutally crushed because she is a Protestant. Despite living in a large family with at least four sisters, he has no realistic idea of women as human beings like himself.

While he is living at Blackrock he daydreams over the idealized figure of Mercedes from *The Count of Monte Cristo*. At first she is merely part of Stephen's self-identification with the hero of Dumas's novel. As he grows into adolescence, her image acquires sexual undertones, although in an unfocused way.

After his family moves to Dublin, Stephen meets a girl named Emma Clery. When they ride home together on a tram after a children's party, she gives him the opportunity to make advances, but Stephen does not follow this through. He remains attracted to Emma throughout the book and composes two poems to her. They are written ten years apart, but neither has anything to do with the real Emma.

Stephen's inability to respond to young women in a natural way drives him in two different directions. On one hand, he uses erotic photographs and nighttime fantasies about Emma to satisfy his lust. (We are given this information later.) On one evening of restless wandering, he meets a prostitute. She takes Stephen back to her room and offers him his first real sexual encounter.

On the other hand, Stephen still has glimpses of an idealized Mercedes. When he starts visiting the brothels on a regular basis, the Blessed Virgin Mary begins to appear in his daydreams. This surprises him, but it should not surprise us. Stephen's idea of "woman" and the figures that embody it slide between two extremes. Neither of them is likely to offer a solution to his problems. By the end of the novel, Stephen takes a slightly more realistic view of Emma, but he can only do this by treating his obsession as one of the ties he must break in order to fly free.

Images, symbols, and "epiphanies"

The **imagery** in *A Portrait* is a great deal denser than in most other novels and is used in several ways. There are repeating pairs of opposites, such as wet/dry, hot/cold, darkness/light, which help to define Stephen's varying moods and the conflicts that experience brings him. Water imagery is especially significant, from the child's reaction when he wets the bed to the adult acceptance of life when Stephen goes to wade in the sea.

There is also **symbolism**. Colors play a large part in this. The red and green colors of Dante's hairbrushes are repeated in the red and green of the Christmas decorations, and both times associated with violent disagreement. Both the cow of Stephen's bedtime story and the color green are symbols of Ireland, and recur at different points in the story.

Stephen is shown crossing bridges at moments of decision, while the flight of birds is associated with his efforts to break away from his environment. Skull imagery is used when Stephen approaches the rector of Clongowes to protest his caning and also when he is asked to consider entering the priesthood. This image is symbolic of what is negative and must be rejected, so that when it is linked with Stephen's friend Cranly, we know that he too must be seen as a hindrance to Stephen's final escape.

Imagery taken from the Daedalus myth has already been discussed above. In fact, the imagery and themes of *A Portrait* are closely intertwined. Both function at a level that is more usually found in lyric verse than in prose fiction. In this sense, and not just for the beauty of its language, *A Portrait* is truly a "poetic" novel. Examining its imagery alone would produce a book as long as *A Portrait* itself. If you answer a question on this aspect, concentrate on one or two examples and follow them through in detail, rather than skimming through a larger number. For example, you might follow through the water or color imagery already mentioned and examine the way the images are used in different incidents. Water is at first associated with cold and slime – everything that is repellent. By the end of the book, in the form of the sea, it represents a positive and energetic attitude toward life. Reread the opening pages of the book for examples you could use.

Epiphany is the word Joyce himself used to describe a moment when some particular experience reveals its inner meaning with an intensity that fixes it in the mind permanently. Joyce borrowed the term from church ritual and gave it this individual meaning.

In *Stephen Hero*, an earlier and much less complex version of *A Portrait*, Joyce described an epiphany as "a sudden spiritual manifestation, whether in the vulgarity of speech or in a memorable phase of the mind itself." Examples are Stephen's tram journey with Emma when *his heart danced in her movements like a cork upon a tide*, his glimpse of the word *Foetus* carved on a desk of the anatomy theater in Cork, and the girl/bird image that confronts him when he wades in the sea.

The epiphanies are, therefore, of two kinds, but whichever group they belong to, they are associated with moments of intense emotion. They are a real-life parallel to the *enchantment of the heart* that Stephen discusses in his theory of aesthetics. The bird/girl epiphany has links with other images and themes in the narrative. ❂ What are they?

The disappearing author

As part of the new techniques mentioned earlier, many of the events in the novel are presented to us not through narrative but indirectly through Stephen's thoughts and feelings. The background to events is communicated in the same way. Sometimes the information is not all given at once. For instance, Emma's "betrayal" of Stephen with the priest is mentioned on one page but not explained fully until several pages later. Look out for other examples of this.

Perhaps the most original feature of *A Portrait* is the variation of language that accompanies each stage of its hero's development. Stephen's earliest memories are recalled in his own babyish words. We are placed at the center of his experience and left to interpret this for ourselves.

Style and vocabulary change to suit Stephen's age. As a schoolboy he has appropriately greater word power and can express abstract ideas. *Decent, fellows, mean, in a wax,* and other Clongowes' slang mingle with the images created by an already rich verbal imagination.

As an adolescent, Stephen is immersed in other people's words, trying to understand life through Dumas, Byron, Shelley, and the liturgy of his church. At other times his thoughts unconsciously fall into the language of books he has read. His penitence for his sexual behavior is expressed in phrases that exactly match the hellfire sermons that inspired it.

Stephen's individual voice begins to emerge when he becomes a student. This is both in a literal sense – we hear much more of Stephen's own words in the last chapter – and in the sense that he formulates something original from the words of others, or his aesthetic theory. Finally, the last section of the novel is a direct transcript from Stephen's diary. Here Joyce employs a literary form in which the novelist is invisible.

Now Try This

? Choose three separate passages from the novel (from Chapters 1, 2, and 4 or 5), which, in your view, indicate Stephen's age from their tone, style, and language – not from their content. Be clear about the reasons for your choice before you go on. Join a group of friends who have each done the same. Take turns asking the group to look at your chosen passages and ask what clues they can find to Stephen's age.

"A *fluid and lambent narrative*"

One of the key features of *A Portrait* is the tension between several sets of opposing forces. These form the structural skeleton of the book and hold it together.

Overall, there is a succession of conflicts between Stephen and his environment. After resolving one problem – or thinking he has – he then has to face another. These conflicts can span single sections or whole chapters. The narrative movement is similar to that of waves that follow one after the other to break on the shore, sometimes overlapping and crossing each other. This is done so skillfully that once one has grasped what Joyce is doing, there is no sense of disruption between one episode and the next. They flow into each other like the scenes in a well-made film. Here are a few examples:

In Chapter 1 Stephen is struggling to fit in with the harsh regime at Clongowes. By the end of the chapter he has become popular with his schoolmates for going to the rector to complain about Father Dolan. Much later (in Chapter 2) he learns that the rector's sympathy was only pretended; the priests had laughed at him behind his back. Within this time span, Stephen's hopes for the Christmas vacation are cruelly shattered by a family quarrel. There is the conflict between his daydreams of family harmony and the reality of his family's poverty. His attempts to overcome the poverty with his prize money end in comic failure. Similarly, the pressures of sexual frustration are relieved by visiting prostitutes, but not for long. Stephen is tripped up by his own sense of guilt.

The examples are from the first half of the book. ✪ What others can you find in the second half?

Another important structural tension is the contrast between Stephen's ongoing absorption in himself and the conversations that surround him. This gives a firm reality to the narrative and also underlines Stephen's alienation from his environment. Two examples are the dialogue at the Christmas dinner in which Stephen himself takes no part except to say grace, and the shouted comments on the beach in Chapter 4.

A *hero in double focus*

The author's withdrawal from his role as "tour guide" (see the section A New Kind of Novel on p. 3) leaves readers freer to interpret his text than some may want to be. If you consult other commentaries on *A Portrait* you will discover that, although all agree on the main distinguishing features of Joyce's writing, they differ markedly in their reactions to Stephen.

This is unusual. There are generally accepted views about Shakespeare's tragic heroes and the heroines of the Russian novelist Tolstoy. This does not mean either that Joyce has drawn his character uncertainly or that the others lack complexity and depth. The difference arises because Joyce has chosen to study the emergence of great artistic talent in someone whose character and perceptions are still not mature enough at the end of the book to allow that talent to flower.

Everyone can identify and sympathize with the terrors and sufferings of a young child. The difficulty begins when Stephen moves into adolescence. His arrogance, egotism, and self-absorption are not attractive features. How far you let them influence your attitude toward him will depend on whether: (*a*) you think he could not have become an artist without the kind of isolation he imposed on himself, and (*b*) you think/don't think the cost he had to pay for this in personal terms was worth it.

By the end of the book Stephen has produced only two poems of no special merit. We have to take it on trust that he will indeed mature into the great artist that he thinks he is.

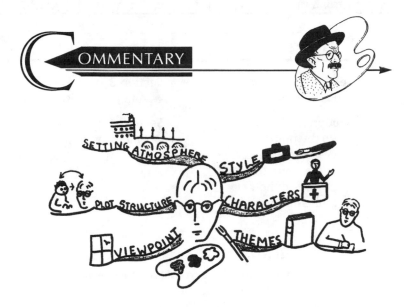

COMMENTARY

To make revision easier, the Commentary divides the chapters into short sections, beginning with a brief preview that will prepare you for the section and help with last-minute revision. The Commentary discusses whatever is important in the section, focusing on the areas shown in the Mini Mind Map above.

ICONS

Wherever the focus is on a particular theme, the icon for that theme appears in the margin (see p. ix for key). Look out, too, for the Style and Language sections. Being able to comment on style and language will help you get an "A" on your exam.

You will learn more from the Commentary if you use it alongside the novel itself. Read a section from the novel, then the corresponding Commentary section – or the other way around.

STARRED QUESTIONS

Remember that when a question appears in the Commentary with a star ✪ in front of it, you should stop and think about it for a moment. And do **remember to take a break** after completing each exercise.

Chapter 1

SECTION 1

Baby Tuckoo

A Portrait of the Artist as a Young Man follows the traditional pattern of autobiographical fiction by beginning with the hero's boyhood. In a strikingly different and original way the memories are described in Stephen's own babyish words. There is no comment or explanation from the writer. The effect is to make us feel we are sharing Stephen's experience as he passes from infancy to childhood.

Stephen's father is telling him a story. Stephen is part of the story – he is the little boy who meets the *moocow*. His father has a hairy face. There is a song he remembers, but he cannot say the words properly. Wetting the bed is at first a pleasure, but then brings discomfort. His mother smells nicer than his father.

Uncle Charles and Dante are part of Stephen's family. Dante has two brushes with different-colored backs. There is another family nearby called the Vances. Stephen will marry Eileen Vance when they are grown up. He is threatened with punishment after some naughty act and hides under the table. His mother says he will apologize. Dante says the eagles will pluck out his eyes if he does not.

These events have no connection with each other. We are not told when they happened or in what order. Stephen finds them all of equal interest. He does not put them in order of importance or, like adults, feel shame at certain types of behavior. His memories are convincing because that is the way we all remember childhood – in vivid pictures and strong physical sensations.

However, the section is more than a set of random images. It contains the whole book in miniature.

Joyce has given his hero his own poor eyesight. The senses of touch, hearing, smell, are even more important to Stephen than they are to most children. Hot and cold, dry and wet, dark and light, noise and silence are some of the opposites that appear in every chapter. These become associated with his states of mind and link the major themes of the novel.

This vivid awareness of his senses will follow Stephen into adult life, part of his gifts as an artist. So too will the fascination with words. His first memory is of being told a story by his father *Once upon a time ...* . Lines of songs and snatches of music loom large in his recollections.

This section also sketches out the conflicts that will dominate Stephen when he is older. He already knows about the campaign for Irish Home Rule through the red and green backs of Dante's brushes. These colors symbolize different aspects of Ireland, the Emerald Isle, with its bloodstained history. The mention of Eileen foreshadows his difficulty in forming relationships with women. Dante's threat of avenging eagles will be reflected later in Stephen's tortured wrestling with sin and repentance.

Try these questions

?   How far back can you remember? How far can your friends go? Make a list of your earliest memories – ten if possible.

?   Compare these with Stephen's. As a very young child, what were you most aware of – colors, sounds, or smells?

Take a break before reading about Stephen's school days

SECTION 2

The best years of his life?

At the age of six Stephen is sent to Clongowes Wood College, a boarding school for boys 20 miles west of Dublin. Joyce himself was a pupil there for a few years. Mr. and Mrs. Dedalus are Roman Catholics so they want their son to have a Catholic education. The college is run by the religious order of the Society of Jesus, which specialized in missionary and educational work. At Clongowes the masters, or "prefects," are all Jesuit priests.

The section opens with evening rugby practice. Stephen is afraid of being hurt, and he is still homesick. His poor eyesight makes him see the game in a blur with occasional details standing out. Joyce uses these to emphasize Stephen's dislike of rough exercise – *the greasy leather orb; the flashing eyes and muddy boots ran after; their legs were rubbing and kicking and stamping.*

A CRUEL SHOCK

Instead of joining in the game, Stephen thinks about the other boys. Their aggressiveness has been a shock after the affectionate pampering of his family.

His mind keeps running between home and school, where he still feels like an outsider. He has recently been pushed into the cesspool by the bully, Wells. Although he doesn't know it yet, he is coming down with a fever. The memory of *cold slimy water next his skin* immediately makes him think of his mother and Dante enjoying tea in front of a warm fire.

❂ What other contrasts of hot and cold are mentioned in this section?

Stephen is continually turning over words and phrases – sentences from his class books, geographical names, and even the school slang. Their rhythm and sound delight him. They also provide an escape from his unpleasant surroundings. He finds another refuge in the romantic history of the school building.

The boys are called inside for Father Arnall's arithmetic lesson. They compete in two teams wearing the red and white rose badges of York and Lancaster.

We can tell that Stephen gets good marks when he concentrates, because there are bets on him to come in first against the other class favorite. But he is already getting sick with a fever. His mind wanders off to the colors of roses.

In the refectory Stephen is disgusted by the pale, damp bread and cannot force himself to eat. One of the boys shows concern, but when they go to the playroom, the bully Wells picks on Stephen again and asks a trick question about whether he kisses his mother goodnight.

During the homework period, Stephen checks off one more day before the Christmas vacation. While trying to study geography, he starts thinking about the immensity of the universe and the mystery of God. Politics, which he associates with the red and green of Dante's brushes, present another mystery.

Stephen longs for bed, but chapel and prayers must be endured first. Images of night, darkness, and cold fill his mind. After undressing he has to say his own personal prayers and *be in bed before the gas was lowered so that he might not go to hell when he died.* He is trembling and shaking uncontrollably. As he falls asleep, tales of the old castle become muddled with chapel prayers and his longing to go home for the Christmas vacation.

STEPHEN BECOMES ILL

In the morning Stephen is so feverish that he has to stay in bed. Before he is taken to the school infirmary, Wells approaches and begs Stephen not to inform on him. Stephen reassures Wells that he won't, and feels *glad.* ❂ Why?

There is another boy named Athy in the infirmary. He jokes with Brother Michael, the infirmary attendant, who reads news items aloud to him from the paper. Athy speaks sympathetically to Stephen, his first friendly encounter at Clongowes.

In the half-waking, half-sleeping state brought on by the fever, Stephen imagines his own death. He is sentimentally moved by thoughts of his requiem mass in the school chapel.

In the evening his fever gets higher. He imagines that the firelight turns into dark, heaving waves, and he sees the ship that is bringing Parnell's body back to Ireland. The mourners on the quayside send up a sorrowful cry as the ship enters the harbor. Dante walks past them in silence wearing green and maroon velvet.

Now answer some questions on the scene in the infirmary

? Look at the conversation between Athy and Stephen. How does Athy try to make Stephen feel at ease?
? What details show that Stephen is sensitive about his family's social background?
? Say how Athy's behavior contrasts with that of the other boys.

now take a break before Stephen's disastrous Christmas

SECTION 3

Christmas dinner

Before you study this section, make sure you understand why the clergy disagreed with Parnell.

A great fire, banked high and red, flamed in the grate. Stephen has returned to his family. For the first time he joins the adults for their Christmas dinner – his parents, Uncle Charles, Dante – Mrs. Riordan – and John Casey, a family friend who was once imprisoned as a rebel against the British occupation of Ireland.

Stephen says grace. He is blissfully happy as they sit down to eat. *Clongowes was far away.* There is hot, appetizing food on the table and the room is cheerful with green and red decorations. This is a picture of the conventionally happy family Christmas.

There is general good will until Mr. Dedalus and John Casey begin to joke about a man who criticized his priest for preaching politics. (The Irish clergy stopped supporting Parnell when they learned about his relationship with Kitty O'Shea.)

Dante speaks up for the priest. He was right to denounce immorality, she says indignantly. Mrs. Dedalus and Uncle Charles manage to calm the dispute, but it flares up again. The others sit silent and embarrassed as the incident turns into a serious quarrel. Mr. Dedalus makes a general attack on churchmen and others who broke *Parnell's heart and hounded him into the grave,* while Dante claims to be defending her religion against *renegade Catholics.*

A VIOLENT QUARREL

Mrs. Dedalus and Uncle Charles remind them that Stephen is present, but by now the quarrel has gone too far for the others to restrain themselves. Mr. Casey is a Parnell supporter. He describes his encounter with a *drunken old harridan* after a political meeting in Arklow. He spins out the story for maximum effect on Dante. The woman was screaming insults at Parnell and Kitty O'Shea, he says. *When she called that lady a name I won't sully this Christmas board ... by repeating,* he spat a mouthful of tobacco juice in her eye.

Stephen is bewildered and distressed by the hostility among the grownups. He likes Mr. Casey but he has been trained to be reverent toward the Church. Why is Mr. Casey attacking the priests? Dante must be right, but his father has told him Dante is a *spoiled nun.* Perhaps that is why she is so much against Parnell. She tried to stop him from playing with his Protestant friend, Eileen. So who was right? Dante used to support Parnell herself. Stephen has seen her use her umbrella to hit a man who took off his hat for *God Save the Queen.*

Dante is enraged by John Casey's story. She and the two men begin shouting at each other. After a few bitter exchanges she storms out of the room. Mr. Dedalus bows his head and sobs. Stephen is terrified as he sees his father's eyes full of tears.

Two questions now about this section

? Who do you think was most responsible for the quarrel at the Christmas dinner?

? Why are families often under a lot of stress at Christmastime? What topics of dispute can arise?

SECTION 4

Injustice and a beating

In the next scene Stephen is back at school. Five of the older students have been caught several miles outside the school grounds. They have been given the choice of flogging or expulsion. Stephen listens to rumors about why they ran away.

They stole money out of the rector's room, says one boy. No, says Wells. They went into the sacristy and drank the altar wine. Stephen is shocked that anyone would break into a room where robes and vessels for the mass are kept.

He can see even less than usual because his glasses have been broken in a collision with a racing cyclist. As Stephen listens to the sound of balls on cricket bats, Athy says that the five ran away because they were caught *smugging* in the square – indulging in sexual play in the water closet (bathroom).

The boys fall silent but Stephen is baffled. He is still ignorant about such matters. *It was a joke, he thought.* He recalls what he knows about "Tusker" Boyle – one of the boys caught – who is *always at his nails, paring them.* This immediately reminds him that Eileen Vance once put her hand inside his pocket and then ran away laughing.

Stephen cannot grasp the meaning of this either and he is too innocent to understand the connection he has made. His encounter with Eileen explains some phrases in the litany of the Blessed Virgin. Eileen's hands are a *Tower of Ivory* and her blonde hair is a *House of Gold.*

The incident also demonstrates Stephen's need to cope with a new experience by wrapping it in romantic verbal associations. When he is older this habit will aggravate his problems in forming relationships with girls.

By thinking of things you could understand them, Stephen reassures himself. His thoughts return to the *square* where the boys are supposed to have committed their acts. He begins to feel afraid. His classmates discuss the details of a school flogging, and Stephen senses that they are afraid too.

They go indoors for a writing lesson. Stephen can hardly see the page, so he is excused and sits with folded arms. He wonders if the five boys have desecrated the altar and is fascinated by the thought of a sin so *terrible and strange*.

When Father Arnall enters to give a Latin lesson, he reprimands the whole class for their bad homework and orders Fleming to kneel on the floor. Stephen is beginning to observe that his teachers do not all live up to the ideals of their Order. Is it a sin for Father Arnall *to be in a wax* (angry) as he so obviously is?

FATHER DOLAN

The prefect of studies enters with his cane to punish anyone who has been lazy. Father Dolan is a bully, far less controlled in his anger than Father Arnall. He threatens the whole class and canes Fleming with relish. Then he jumps on Stephen. Although the teacher backs up Stephen's story about breaking his glasses, Father Arnall *pandies* him once on each hand.

The pain is even worse than he imagined. At the second blow Stephen cannot hold back his cries and tears. He is in a state of shock that makes him detach what he feels from the actual sight of his swollen, beaten hands, as if they belonged to someone else. Full of shame and rage, he relives the experience during the rest of the lesson.

Stephen's classmates share his indignation at the unjust treatment. They tell him to go to the rector and complain. One of the older boys humorously quotes a formula used to introduce decrees of the ancient Roman senate. Stephen, however, picks it up in earnest. With a mixture of self-importance and real courage, he decides that he will go to the rector after dinner.

While he is eating, Stephen is tortured by indecision. He is afraid the rector may side with Father Dolan. Nevertheless he forces himself to leave the others at the end of the meal and walk along the dark, narrow corridor that leads to the rector's apartment. His route is lined with portraits of eminent men associated with the Jesuit order. A servant tells him which door to knock at.

The solemnity of the room is overwhelming, but the rector has a kindly manner and he believes Stephen's story, although he also finds a way to excuse Father Dolan's behavior.

This release of tension throws Stephen into a state of wild excitement. He rushes back to his classmates to tell them what has happened. They burst into cheers and hoist him shoulder high. For the first time he feels at peace at Clongowes, fully accepted into the community.

A final question on Chapter 1

? Look back at the section on Themes (p. 21) and choose two. How have they been developed in this chapter?

Stephen's family circumstances begin to deteriorate – after the break

Chapter 2

Section 1
◆ "Training" at Blackrock
◆ The Count of Monte Cristo

Section 2
◆ Dublin relations
◆ Emma Clery
◆ "Father Dolan and I had a hearty laugh"

Section 3
◆ The Whitsuntide play
◆ Admit! Admit!
◆ No Emma

Section 4
◆ A visit to Cork

Section 5
◆ How Stephen spent his prize money
◆ Mercedes at last?

SECTION 1

Blackrock

Chapter 2 covers five episodes from Stephen's life up to the age of 16. When it opens the family has moved from Bray to Blackrock and Stephen himself is on the verge of adolescence. The Dedalus family is about to be reduced to real poverty.

Stephen's school has closed for the summer vacation. This is the period in his life when he seems most involved with his family and most willing to follow the path laid out for him.

Every morning he helps Uncle Charles shop for household groceries. Afterwards they go to the park to meet Mike Flynn, who, according to his father, is a top-ranked athletics trainer. Mike Flynn's *flabby stubble covered face ... mild lustreless blue eyes* and *long swollen fingers* make Stephen think this claim unlikely, but he follows Mike's instructions as he runs around the park. On the way home, Stephen and Uncle Charles visit the chapel and Stephen kneels at his great-uncle's side *respecting, though he did not share, his piety.*

❂ What do these examples of daily routine tell us about Stephen's present attitude toward his family?

THE COUNT OF MONTE CRISTO

Stephen is reading Dumas's *The Count of Monte Cristo.* In the role of Edmond Dantes he lives out imaginary adventures *marvellous as those in the book itself.* A house near Blackrock is the home of the faithless Mercedes, whom he enjoys rejecting.

In real life Stephen roams about with a gang of boys headed by himself and his friend, Aubrey Mills. He and Aubrey accompany the milkman when he drives into the country to fill his churns. In the fall the cows are brought back to a village yard. Stephen is revolted by the mess and stink they create in the confined space.

He does not return to Clongowes for the next school term. Stephen realizes that his father is in financial trouble and notices the changes in their standard of living. The insecurity this causes makes him shrink back into himself.

To fill up time he accompanies the milkman on his evening rounds. He stares inquisitively into the houses they stop at and thinks this might be a pleasant enough life for him. But he knows that his future is uncertain. *The ambition which he felt astir at times in the darkness of his soul sought no outlet.*

Stephen broods about his vision of Mercedes. In the evening he wanders around the neighborhood to quiet his *strange unrest.* Although he takes no practical steps to satisfy these yearnings, he feels sure that one day he will *meet in the real world the unsubstantial image which his soul so constantly beheld.* In an instant he will be able to put aside *weakness and timidity and inexperience.*

See what more you have discovered about Stephen

? Why do you think Stephen has so little feeling of conflict with his family at this point, compared with his later situation?

? What is your reaction to Stephen's feelings? Are any of the words below appropriate? What others might you use instead?

unrealistic   shy   sensitive   pathetic   romantic
childish   naive   tender   extravagant   fanciful
deluded   foolish   worshipful   adoring   confused
inexperienced

give yourself a break before moving on to Stephen's meeting with Emma Clery

SECTION 2

A *new life in Dublin*

The Dedalus family has now moved into the center of Dublin. Mr. Dedalus tries to keep up the family's spirits with empty, boastful talk, but their poverty cannot be hidden. Stephen explores the new environment timidly at first, and then more boldly as the city streets become familiar to him. The area of docks and quays reminds him of Mercedes.

His mother takes him to visit some Dublin relatives. To Stephen these people are strangers whom he resents having to spend time with. He is angry at his own discontent and feels humiliated by his father's loss of income. His way of coping is to detach himself from the situation and not show his anger in public. This self-control will become even greater in the next section when he is dealing with the "ragging" of his new schoolmates.

Two visits to relatives are described. Stephen's aunt and cousin are staring fascinated at a picture of a beautiful actress in the evening paper. A boy enters with a sack of coals and grabs the paper with his grimy hands.

Stephen is imagining pictures in the fire as he listens to his mother and an elderly woman discussing a simple-minded girl. Suddenly she appears, *a skull ... suspended in the gloom of the doorway. A feeble creature like a monkey.*

Both these visits end with "epiphanies," but of a kind different from the famous image of the wading girl in the newspaper. These two – and the image of the man with the *blackish monkey-puckered face* – are a revelation of what Stephen feels contempt for, most obviously when the word *beautiful* is linked to a coal-grimed newspaper illustration. It need hardly be said that these are *Stephen's* opinions, and Stephen is both snobbish and intellectually arrogant.

In the third scene Stephen is at a children's party at Harold's Cross. He is young enough to be invited but too old to enjoy the youngsters' romping until he has withdrawn from them and become a spectator.

EMMA – A MISSED OPPORTUNITY

He is conscious that Emma Clery is trying to catch his eye, *flattering, taunting, searching, exciting his heart.* They take the last tram home together and are the only passengers. Emma stands on the step below Stephen and makes open advances to him. Here is a real-life chance to fulfill his fantasy, but he is unable to seize his opportunity. He lets Emma get off the tram, unkissed. When she is gone Stephen tears his ticket into shreds and stares gloomily at the floor.

The next day he writes a poem about his experience. He remembers a previous occasion – the aftermath of the Christmas family quarrel – when he tried to do this and failed. This time he is successful. He gazes admiringly at himself in his mother's mirror, pleased that he has erased everything *common and insignificant* from the poem. His verses tell *only of the night and the balmy breeze and the maiden lustre of the moon*. The young artist who observes the world in such detail has not yet realized that the "common and insignificant" will give life to his art.

NOT SUCH A HERO

One evening Mr. Dedalus comes home with important news. He has met Father Conmee, the rector of Clongowes, and has arranged for Stephen and his younger brother, Maurice, to attend Belvedere, the Jesuits' day school in Dublin. Stephen's parents are delighted – the alternative was to send their sons to a school run by the Christian Brothers, which has a much lower social status. Look back at the lines: *It was his own name ... washed clothes.* ❂ What does this reveal to us about Stephen's own social attitudes?

Mr. Dedalus is in a very good mood. The rector has told him about his interview with Stephen after he was *pandied* by Father Dolan. *Manly little chap* was his comment. Unfortunately, Mr. Dedalus does not have the good sense to finish his story there. He goes on to say that the two Jesuits made a joke of the whole affair. *I told them all at dinner about it and Father Dolan and I and all of us we had a hearty laugh together.*

Now answer these questions

? What does this incident tell us about (a) Mr. Dedalus, (b) Stephen's teachers?

? What does Mr. Dedalus mean when he says, *O, a Jesuit for your life, for diplomacy!*

? How do you think Stephen felt when his father told this story?

? What effect would it have on his attitude toward his father and his teachers?

next – another shock for Stephen – but first recharge your batteries

SECTION **3**

The Whitsuntide play

The narrative now moves forward about two years. Stephen has settled in well at his new school. The Belvedere pupils are putting on a performance for friends and parents. In the dressing room Stephen watches the younger boys prepare for the dance and gymnastics exhibition. He himself has a leading role in a play that will be presented later that evening.

When he goes out to the garden, the strains of a waltz played by the school orchestra stir up the feelings that have agitated him all day. He has a conversation with his classmate, Heron, who has stepped outside with a friend to smoke.

Heron teases Stephen about Emma Clery – the cause of his unrest; Heron has overheard her talking to Stephen's father and calls Stephen *a sly dog*. Stephen dislikes both the reference to his father and the talk about Emma, who is now the focus of strong sexual attraction for him.

HOW STEPHEN STOOD UP FOR HIMSELF

Yet his anger is brief; he knows they cannot enter his mind. When Heron strikes his leg, crying *Admit!* he diverts their curiosity with a mock *Confiteor* (confession). He is reminded of a similar incident in his first term at Belvedere, when the English teacher accused him of heresy (holding a different opinion to that of the accepted doctrine), a grave sin for a Catholic student. The teacher was satisfied when he retracted by altering some words in his essay.

Stephen's classmates pursued the point with *a vague general malignant joy*, perhaps because they liked seeing know-it-all Stephen get into trouble. They approached him one evening and pestered him to name the best poet. When Stephen claimed that Byron was a better poet than Tennyson, they tried to beat out of him the admission that Byron was *no good* since he was *a heretic and immoral too.*

Stephen remembers that he refused to give in to their bullying although it reduced him to tears. Since then he has learned to rely on the *intangible phantoms* of his inner life to resist the pressures that urge him to be a good Catholic, a gentleman, to follow the schoolboy code of honor, and devote himself to his family and country. ❷ How does his attitude here compare with the way he felt at Blackrock?

Stephen is called inside to be made up for his part in the play. Some of the lines cause him acute embarrassment, but the thought that Emma will be watching him makes him feel confident. For once in his life Stephen feels like a member of the group. Ironically this occurs when everyone is projecting a false identity as a character in a play. *The excitement and youth about him ... transformed his moody mistrustfulness. For one rare moment he seemed to be clothed in the real apparel of boyhood: and, as he stood in the wings among the other players he shared the common mirth.*

ANOTHER DISAPPOINTMENT

When the play is over Stephen hurries to get out of his costume and then rushes into the hall to look for Emma. He finds his family waiting for him outside, but Emma is not with them. Bitterly disappointed, he makes an excuse to leave them and runs across the road trying to leave behind the chaos of his feelings. Near the river he suffers another violent change of mood. As he comes to a halt, his passion burns itself out. The rank smell of the mortuary stables has a calming effect on him and he returns home.

Now Try This

? How do you think Stephen's classmates found out about his interest in Emma?

? What does Joyce mean by *the real apparel of boyhood*?

SECTION **4**

A *visit to Cork*

Mr. Dedalus returns to his native Cork to sell off the remainder of the family property. He takes Stephen with him. This fourth section concentrates on the father–son relationship, which, from Stephen's point of view, is highly unsatisfactory. Mr. Dedalus is unaware of his own shortcomings as a father.

✪ Ask yourself whether the faults are all on one side. Stephen is so self-absorbed that he will not share his feelings with anyone. How does his resentment about his circumstances compare with that of a teenager whose parents "do not understand him?"

On their night train journey Stephen listens coldly to his father rambling on about the friends and scenes of his youth. He realizes that the purpose of their journey will have a serious effect on him personally. *In the manner of his own dispossession he felt the world give the lie rudely to his phantasy.*

In their sunny hotel room Mr. Dedalus perks up and sings as he studies his face and hair in the mirror. At breakfast his questions put him at cross purposes with the waiter because the names he mentions signify another generation to the younger man.

Father and son visit Queen's College, Mr. Dedalus's old university, and are shown around by the college porter. Stephen is thrown into a fever of impatience as the two men stop after every few steps to discuss some former acquaintance. He can see that the porter is humoring Mr. Dedalus, no doubt hoping for a large tip at the end, and is surprised that his father can be so gullible.

In the anatomy lecture hall, the porter helps Mr. Dedalus search for his initials. Stephen hangs around gloomily in the background. Suddenly his eyes light on a word carved several times into a desk – *Foetus*. He withdraws in horror, interpreting this as a link with the *monstrous reveries* – sexual dreams and fantasies – that had *sprung up before him, suddenly and furiously, out of mere words.*

47

STEPHEN IS CONSUMED WITH GUILT

Until then Stephen has assumed that his adolescent imaginings are unique to himself. Finding that others do the same does not bring any reassurance. On the contrary, he is overwhelmed with guilt and self-loathing for *his mad and filthy orgies*.

As they stroll around the town, Mr. Dedalus gives his son some good-humored advice. He believes that Stephen and he are more like brothers than father and son, just the way his own father treated him. Stephen is not listening. He feels that his *monstrous way of life* has put him out of touch with reality and tries to get a grip on it again by reciting his name and other details. He has lost even his memories of childhood. The person he was then has *faded out like a film in the sun*.

After the property has been auctioned off, Stephen follows his father around the pubs of Cork, where Mr. Dedalus goes on a prolonged drinking spree. To Stephen's embarrassment he becomes more and more talkative. He flirts and boasts and publicly compares himself with his son – much to his own advantage. Stephen is deeply ashamed of his father, while at the same time aware that he himself has missed out by being incapable of such simple enjoyment. *He had known neither the pleasure of companionship with others nor the vigor of rude male health nor filial piety*. He compares himself to the *barren shell* of the moon in Shelley's poem.

Stephen's attitude to his own sexuality

? What do you think of Stephen's view of himself at this stage? Is he overdramatizing his sense of guilt, taking himself too seriously, exaggerating his *monstrous reveries*, being too hard on himself?

? What causes him to react this way? Would you put it down to his education or his inward-looking temperament, or both?

Take a break before Stephen finds some temporary relief to his problems

SECTION 5

How Stephen spent his money

There are two episodes in this last section of Chapter 2. Each concentrates on one of two problems obsessing Stephen at this time – his family's lack of money, and sex.

Poverty, like wealth, is relative. In the 1880s and 1890s, servants were employed even in quite low-income households. Nevertheless, it is evident from the description of the family Christmas dinner (Chapter 1, Section 3) that the Dedalus family enjoys a good standard of living. As Stephen grows up, this standard begins to decline. In this context we should not judge the decline by our own ideas of "well-off" or "poor," but in terms of the insecurity caused by any change for the worse, and its effect on a sensitive child.

Stephen wins an exhibition and essay competition. He collects his prize money of £33 – a considerable amount in those days – from a bank that had once housed the Irish Parliament. Mr. Dedalus, as usual, is reminded of the glory days of old while Stephen is impatient to spend his money.

STEPHEN'S SPENDING SPREE

He takes his family out to dinner in one of Dublin's best restaurants. Afterwards, he plans *a form of commonwealth for the household by which every member of it held some office.* His mother gently tries to restrain his extravagance, but the theater outings and deliveries of luxury food continue until the money is all spent.

❂ Are you surprised at Stephen's generosity? The paragraph beginning *How foolish his aim had been ...* shows that one of his motives was to bridge the gap between himself and his family. Another was to subdue his sexual fantasies. At the end of the spending spree, Stephen realizes he is unable to control either *the sordid tide of life without* (outside) *him* or *the tides within.* ❂ Why do you think these two aspects are so closely connected in his mind?

At this point he is about 16 years old. He is tormented both by physical lust and by guilt at his desperate attempts to satisfy it.

His fantasies are projected onto a figure that by day is *demure and innocent* and by night *transfigured by a lecherous cunning ... eyes bright with brutish joy.* These moments alternate with another extreme – the idealized image of Mercedes in her small white house surrounded by its garden of rosebushes.

MERCEDES AT LAST

Stephen takes to roaming the streets at night *like some baffled prowling beast.* ❍ Is this another exaggeration? Eventually, he wanders into the red light district of Dublin and sees the brightly dressed prostitutes sauntering up and down the road and standing in doorways. They are *leisurely and perfumed.*

STYLE AND LANGUAGE

A young woman accosts him and takes him home. Notice how the details of the encounter and the way she treats Stephen highlight the unreality of his fantasies. The prostitute's room is *warm and lightsome* and she has a doll sitting in a chair. Far from exulting in sin, she approaches Stephen with *serious calm* and *frank uplifted eyes.* She calls him a *little rascal* as she ruffles his hair. Although they are probably much the same age, her attitude toward Stephen is almost maternal. Stephen wants *to be held firmly in her arms, to be caressed slowly.* He feels he is *strong and fearless and sure of himself* – a detail from the more idealistic side of his fantasies – but he finds himself unable to give her the kiss she asks for. The girl has to take the initiative.

Round off this chapter

? Read the sentence: *Stephen looked at his thinly clad mother ... windows of Barnardo's.* Is Stephen's thought prompted by generosity? Is generosity the motive behind what he does for other members of his family? Why doesn't he buy the coat for his mother?

? How would you describe the contrast between Stephen's fantasies about Mercedes and the reality of his encounter with the prostitute?

Chapter 3

SECTION 1

A *short-lived balance*

Stephen is at a mathematics lesson but his mind is only half occupied with the equation in front of him. He is anxiously looking forward to his evening meal, followed by another visit to the brothel area. These visits now seem to be an established habit. *He had sinned mortally not once but many times.*

While he works through the mathematical problem, Stephen examines his own state of mind and conscience. His encounter with the prostitute has established *a dark peace* between body and soul. The knowledge that he is in a state of sin brings only a *cold lucid indifference.* He sees his soul *unfolding itself sin by sin* in the same way as the equation expands in his notebook, and he compares both with the *vast circle of starry life.* Stephen feels contempt for less bright classmates and the adults who listen to mass outside the church on Sunday mornings. He knows his behavior is unfitting for someone who is a prefect in the sodality of the Blessed Virgin Mary, yet *the falsehood of his position did not pain him.* Any impulse to confess is quenched immediately when he looks at his classmates' faces. ✪ Why?

He takes sensuous pleasure in the *glories of Mary* and the litanies he reads aloud. The sin that separates him from God has drawn him closer to the *refuge of sinners*. (In Catholic doctrine, Mary's pleas have more strength than those of other intercessors such as the saints.) Mary's *mild pity* comforts Stephen; he also dwells with some relish on the fact that he turns to her immediately after giving in to lust.

✪ How do you explain this? Perhaps his *dark peace* is more fragile than he thinks. He is still going from one extreme to another, as when he alternated between lustful fantasy and an impossibly idealized Mercedes.

After the lesson ends, the class waits for the rector to arrive and test them on the catechism. Stephen reflects on other sins that his lust has led him into. It gives him *an arid pleasure* to analyze them through obscure points of church doctrine and *feel the more deeply his own condemnation.*

The rector enters. Instead of catechizing them, he announces a three-day retreat in honor of St. Francis Xavier. This will involve rigorous soul-searching, confession, and communion.

Stephen's heart began slowly to fold and fade with fear like a withering flower.

Test your understanding

?   *His senses, stultified only by his desire, would note keenly all that wounded or shamed them.* What is the underlying meaning of this sentence? Is it (*a*) that even in these circumstances Stephen retains his powers of observation, or (*b*) that he needs to look down on the women to remain in control of the situation, or (*c*) that he is trying to exaggerate his own wickedness, or (*d*) something else?

?   How do you explain the sudden overturning of Stephen's self-confidence?

Take a rest before reading about the retreat sermons

SECTION 2

Death and judgment

The retreat sermons are to be given by Father Arnall, a priest from Clongowes. At the sight of his old teacher Stephen's *soul ... became again a child's soul*, that is, he reverts to the submissive, believing attitude of his early school days. From this incident we can see that Stephen's religious background acts as an even greater barrier to his self-discovery than family or country.

Father Arnall begins by praising St. Francis Xavier and explains the meaning of a retreat. He intends to preach about the four last things – death, judgment, hell, and heaven. He urges the boys to banish all worldly thoughts from their hearts and concentrate on these alone.

Stephen walks home in a state of deep depression. The mutton stew – earlier anticipated with gusto – is eaten with *surly appetite* and it leaves a *thick scum* in his mouth. He feels a *dull fear* and apparently does not go out that evening.

The next day brought death and judgment. After yesterday's mild beginning, Father Arnall describes the horrors of death and burial followed by the sentence awaiting sinners at God's judgment seat.

STYLE AND LANGUAGE

Notice the way the first half of this sermon is given to us as if Stephen were recalling the preacher's words and going over them in his mind. One might suppose this reported style would deaden the grim message. On the contrary, the strength of it lies in its effect on Stephen. Even at this early stage Father Arnall tends to "go over the top." Without the accompaniment of Stephen's reaction we might lose the full impact of his preaching or even find it comic.

Once the mood is established, the Last Judgment is presented by the preacher directly and in words taken from the Book of Revelations. The effect on Stephen is profound. He walks home stricken with shame. His thoughts take on the same ringing, elevated style as the priest's rhetoric.

Stephen is particularly ashamed of the *brutelike lust* that he has associated with his thoughts of Emma. Despite his real-life experiences, he is still conjuring up unrealistic images of *harlots with gleaming jewel eyes*. He tries to obliterate the memory of his fantasies with yet another fantasy – a vision of himself and Emma standing hand in hand in front of the Blessed Virgin.

Hellfire threatens

On the second day of the retreat, Father Arnall begins on a moderate note. After reminding his audience of the fall of Adam and Eve, he outlines the life of Christ. Then he launches into a horrific description of the physical torments of hell – immobility, burning heat, and unbearable noise and stench. Brains boil in their skull, and bowels are a red-hot mass of burning pulp.

We have seen on many occasions how strongly Stephen reacts to sensory experience. He absorbs the preacher's images so intensely that when he passes along a corridor cloakroom, the dripping coats turn into a row of *gibbeted malefactors*. At one point he believes he has died and is actually in hell. He is roused by the sound of voices in the classroom.

❂ Do you think the other boys reacted to Father Arnall's sermon on hell the same way that Stephen did?

STEPHEN DECIDES TO MAKE HIS CONFESSION

Confessions now begin in the chapel. Stephen knows he must seek forgiveness, but he cannot face revealing his sins in the company of his fellow students, even though the confessional is private. He decides he will confess to a priest not connected with the school.

Later that day – toward the end of the afternoon – there is another sermon. According to the plan set up by Father Arnall, this should be on the joys of heaven. The priest announces that he will spend *a few moments* on the spiritual torments of hell. These are analyzed at great length under several different headings. The sermon ends with a reminder of the love and forgiveness of God. The priest and congregation recite an act of contrition together.

Put yourself in Stephen's position

? Why is Stephen unwilling to make his confession at the school?

? Why do you suppose Joyce gives such a large part of this chapter to the retreat sermons?

? What is the significance of the fact that Father Arnall never gets around to describing the joys of heaven?

? How do you think you would have reacted if you had been present at the retreat?

you certainly deserve a break now!

SECTION 3

"The leprous company of his sins"

After the evening meal Stephen goes up to his room and kneels beside his bed *like a child saying his evening prayers*. Full of guilt and fear, he cannot tell the difference between imagination and reality. He gets into bed and huddles miserably under the blankets. *The leprous company of his sins* seem to prowl around him and draw suffocatingly near. This hallucination merges into a nightmare as he falls asleep. He wakes up in terror and vomits into the washbasin.

Compare this passage with the one in Chapter 1, *His fingers trembled ... light was lowered quietly.* ○ What similarities can you find?

When he recovers from his nausea, Stephen prays to the Blessed Virgin and weeps for his lost innocence, then he leaves the house to search for a confessor. He tries to understand why he has sinned. Does his body have a lower soul of its own? He rejects the temptation of this belief – his soul has to take the responsibility for his sinful acts; the body is only its tool.

IN THE CONFESSIONAL

Stephen asks for directions to a chapel. There, waiting his turn to go into the confessional, he kneels among *the humble followers of Jesus ... bidding his heart be meek ... like those who knelt beside him.* Even at his most repentant, Stephen still shares his father's snobbery.

He resists an impulse to leave before his turn and when he enters the confessional runs through all his other sins before reluctantly confessing his *squalid stream of vice.* The Capuchin priest imposes a light penance that Stephen performs before leaving the chapel.

Stephen goes home *conscious of an invisible grace pervading and making light his limbs.* He is uplifted with happiness and amazed by the beauty of *white puddings and eggs and sausages and cups of tea.* He feels his body and soul have been purified and henceforward he will *live in grace a life of peace and virtue and forbearance with others.*

Understand Stephen's reactions

? Why is Stephen so afraid to go into his room?
? Is this the normal reaction of a 16-year-old, even one who feels genuine guilt?
? What does Stephen's behavior in his room tell us about his relationship with his religion?
? How convincing do you find Stephen's repentance?

before studying the results of Stephen's repentance, take a break

Chapter 4

Section 1
◆ St. Stephen?

Section 2
◆ "The Reverend Stephen Dedalus, S.J."?

Section 3
◆ The girl on the shore

SECTION *1*

St. Stephen?

Stephen's behavior changes markedly after his confession and absolution. Every minute of his day is occupied by the contemplation of *some holy image or mystery* and his daily life is laid out in devotional areas. He performs spiritual exercises for the benefit of souls in Purgatory even more zealously than recommended by the Church. He feels that his efforts are being rung up like sums of money on *a great cash register in heaven.*

STYLE AND LANGUAGE

In this section Joyce is poking gentle fun at his hero's earnestness by imitating the solemn style of **hagiography**, that is, the lives of saints and martyrs. Here is an extract from one such biography.

> Many times it was his chance to come to such poor houses as, for want of chimnies, were unbearable for the smoke, yet himself would sit there for three or four hours together when none of his servants were able to abide in the house. And in some other poor houses where stairs were wanting, he would never disdain to climb up a ladder.
>
> H. S. Bowden, *Mementoes of the Martyrs and Confessors of England and Wales,* 1961

The **parody** is kept up until the end of the section. At times the **satire** becomes quite broad, as in the passage where Stephen finds it easier to accept the baffling nature of the Trinity *by reason of their august incomprehensibility.* His attempts to mortify each and every one of his senses are equally comic. Yet there is also pathos in this picture of a healthy adolescent *trying to undo the sinful past* by blocking out his natural responses to life.

These repeated acts of self-suppression drive Stephen even farther away from reality. *The world for all its solid substance and complexity no longer existed for his soul save as a theorem of divine power and love and universality.* He believes he cannot grasp the meaning of love and hate; he has experienced only lust and brief bursts of anger. Neither has ever become *an abiding passion.*

❍ Do you agree with Stephen's judgment of himself?

He is naively surprised that *at the end of his course of intricate piety and self-restraint* there are still small things – for example, the sound of his mother sneezing – that can annoy him. He finds it hard not to show his irritation and is humiliated to remember how his teachers showed the same kind of annoyance toward their students.

Stephen's constant failure *to merge his life in the common tide of other lives* discourages him so much that he begins to doubt whether he really is in a state of grace. He plunges further into unreality; old sacred books and solitary prayers now touch his feelings more than joining others to take communion, the *actual reception of the eucharist.*

Sexual desire begins to tempt him again. He imagines it as the sea advancing in small wavelets toward his naked feet, but he withdraws in time and feels *a new thrill of satisfaction and power* that he has not *yielded sinful consent.* This happens so often that Stephen begins to wonder whether grace is *being filched from him little by little* or whether his first confession to the Capuchin priest had not been valid. He reassures himself; after all, his way of life is utterly changed. Surely that must be a sign of sincere repentance?

Two questions on Stephen's repentance

? Stephen has already been given a penance by the Capuchin priest. Why does he feel the need to impose his own as well?

? What does he hope to achieve by such rigid self-discipline? Would you say it is positive (likely to produce some benefit), or merely negative (intended to prevent him sinning again)?

pause here before reading how Stephen begins to rebel

SECTION 2

The Reverend Stephen Dedalus, S.J.?

Stephen has been summoned by the school director to discuss whether he has a vocation to enter the priesthood. Trying to put Stephen at ease, the director begins by talking about other matters. He makes a sneering remark about the long robes of the Capuchins.

Stephen is embarrassed by the priest's flippancy. He feels he is being tested for his reaction and remembers that the Jesuits have a reputation for being sly. He has not experienced this himself and has always shown his schoolmasters *quiet obedience.* Lately he has begun to find some of their opinions a little childish. Now some *masked memories* return to him of events he did not fully understand at the time.

The director's tone becomes more direct and serious as he comes to the point of the interview. He asks Stephen whether he has ever wished to join the Order – that is, to become a priest in the Society of Jesus. Stephen replies that he has *sometimes thought of it.* The director reminds him that the priesthood is the highest honor God can bestow on a man. Stephen vividly recalls his fantasies of carrying out that role. The rituals performed by a priest attract him *by reason of their semblance of reality and of their distance from it.* ✪ What does Stephen mean by this phrase? The secret knowledge of *obscure things, hidden from others,* and the insight into other people's lives is another powerful attraction.

The director finishes by reminding Stephen that he must be quite sure he has a vocation before he commits himself. As he opens the door to let Stephen out he offers his hand *as if already to a companion in the spiritual life.*

About this interview

? *He had received only two pandies.* How does this compare with the way Stephen felt at the time about the caning he received from Father Dolan? How do you account for the difference?

? What would you say is missing from Stephen's view of a priest's function?

*C*rossing the bridge

Out in the street four young men are striding along to the sound of their leader's concertina. The music dissolves Stephen's fantasies of priesthood *as a sudden wave dissolves the sandbuilt turrets of children.* He imagines his life as a member of the Jesuit community and the thought repels him. At the Jesuit house in Gardiner Street he realizes that he has already chosen not to take up the director's invitation; the loss of freedom would be too great.

On his way home Stephen crosses a bridge, a symbolic event that will be repeated in the next chapter. He looks coldly back at the shrine of the Blessed Virgin standing by a group of cottages. The stink of rotting cabbages meets him as he nears his home. Inside, everything shows that the family has sunk into a state of deep poverty. His brothers and sisters are drinking *second watered tea* out of jam jars; crusts of bread are strewn over the bare boards of the table.

Stephen feels a pang of remorse. Although he has been better treated than his brothers and sisters, they are not jealous of him. They tell Stephen that Mr. and Mrs. Dedalus have gone out to look at another house. The family is about to be evicted again for not paying the rent.

The children begin to sing in chorus, as they often do for hours on end. Stephen joins in, realizing with pain that *even before they set out on life's journey they seemed already weary of the way.* Their voices echo *the recurring note of weariness and pain* in endless generations of children.

This is one of the few times we see Stephen moved by anything like everyday human warmth. ✪ Can you think of other instances? See if you can find one in this section.

Think carefully

? What are Stephen's reasons for rejecting his chance to become a priest?

you are approaching the major turning point of the book. Take a break

SECTION 3

The girl on the shore

Stephen's thoughts have now turned to a university career, and he is waiting impatiently to hear the result of his father's interview with a university tutor. Mr. Dedalus supports Stephen's wishes; as a devout Catholic mother, Mrs. Dedalus is disappointed that Stephen has turned down the opportunity to enter the priesthood. Stephen knows that his decision will cause *the first noiseless sundering of their lives.*

He is exhilarated and eager to plunge into his new life. Too restless to wait any longer for his father, he sets out toward the sea. On the wooden bridge linking Dollymount and the Bull he meets a group of Christian Brothers going in the opposite direction. Stephen is still not completely at ease with his new freedom and feels embarrassed by the encounter. He defends himself by reciting a favorite phrase and thinking about the fascination of words. ❂ Why is Stephen made uncomfortable by his meeting with the Christian Brothers?

STYLE AND LANGUAGE

He passed from the trembling bridge on to dry land again. As in the last section, the bridge image carries a double meaning, being both a description of an actual physical structure and a symbol of significant change. Stephen is walking directly toward the sea, a symbol for the chaos and temptations of life that he will gladly embrace when he rejects the stifling constraints of his boyhood. The water darkens as he looks at it, but he does not turn back. The clouds drifting above him are *hosts of nomads on the march,* reminding him of the lands and peoples of Europe beyond the Irish Sea.

Stephen is hailed by shouts from his friends who are diving off the rocks. The bathers' nakedness revives the guilt and shame he feels for *the mystery of his own body*. Nevertheless, he replies good-humoredly and sits down on a stone block nearby. Their repeated shouts to him remind him of the myth of Daedalus – *the fabulous artificer*.

STEPHEN'S VISION

Stephen has a vision of *a winged form flying above the waves and slowly climbing the air ... a hawklike man flying sunward above the sea*. This image reveals to him *a prophecy of the end he has been born to serve,* his vocation as an artist. To fulfill himself, Stephen realizes, he must accept the call of life. In an instant of ecstatic emotion, he escapes out of adolescence into adulthood.

Make sure you have a thorough knowledge of the myth of Daedalus, or you will miss several significant details in this section. Daedalus is a symbol of the artistic imagination soaring above the earth, but the cries of Stephen's friends – *"Duck him!"*, *"O, cripes I'm drownded!"* and the reference to grave clothes, tell us that we are meant to find parallels in the whole myth, not just the flight of Daedalus. When his son Icarus flew too near the sun, he fell into the sea and was *drownded*. Stephen is both Daedalus and Icarus.

In his exalted state Stephen burns *to set out for the ends of the earth*. He paddles barefoot among the seaweed along a *rivulet in the strand*. There he catches sight of a girl standing in midstream, who reminds him of *a strange and beautiful seabird*. She has tucked her skirts above her knees to keep them out of the water, and her legs are exposed as far as her thighs that are *softhued as ivory*. ✪ Where has ivory been mentioned before, and with what is it associated?

The girl feels Stephen's eyes upon her and she returns his gaze *without shame or wantonness*. Stephen's *outburst of profane joy* springs from his realization that he can appreciate the girl's beauty as an ideal and universal image and at the same time respond to her immediate physical attraction without guilt.

Until now Stephen has channeled his sexual feelings either into idealized fantasy about Mercedes and the Blessed Virgin, or guilt-ridden anonymous encounters in Dublin brothels. Through the girl in the stream he has discovered "the beauty of mortal conditions" (a phrase from *Stephen Hero*). He now realizes that the ideal does not exist separately from everyday reality. This discovery applies to all areas of Stephen's life, but since his most painful problems concern his sexuality, this is the dominant note in his encounter with the girl.

STEPHEN FINDS HIS DESTINY

Stephen has his own particular brand of reality. The *call of life to his soul* rejects not just *the inhuman voice that had called him to the pale service of the altar*, but also *the dull gross world of duties and despair*. ✪ What do you think he is referring to in the last quotation? *Duties and despair* form a large part of most people's idea of reality.

After he sees the girl in the stream Stephen's euphoria takes him striding along the beach. Her image has *passed into his soul for ever*. She is a *wild angel* sent to him to reveal his destiny: to experience life to the full and re-create it in art.

In a state of mystic exaltation, Stephen lies down *amid a ring of tufted sandknolls* to *still the riot in his blood*. There he falls into a rapturous sleep in which he feels his soul *swooning into some new world, fantastic, dim, uncertain as under sea, traversed by cloudy shapes and beings*.

A final thought

? This seems to be a good point to examine the sea/water imagery used in the novel. Begin by finding one example in Section 3. Why is this particularly appropriate for the moment when Stephen realizes he cannot join the priesthood? Collect three or four more examples and discuss them with your friends.

award yourself another break before looking at Stephen, the university student

Chapter 5

Section 1
◆ Stephen & Co.
◆ Conversation with the dean
◆ "I shall try to fly by those nets"
◆ What is beauty?

Section 2
◆ "O what sweet music"

Section 3
◆ Preparing for flight

Section 4
◆ Stephen's diary

SECTION 1

Stephen & Co.

This chapter opens on a very different scene. Stephen is looking at some pawnshop tickets over breakfast. He is late for his university lectures. Evidently this happens quite often, for his mother and one of his sisters try to cover up for him when Mr. Dedalus shouts downstairs, angrily demanding to know whether Stephen is still in the house. Stephen takes this coolly, but once outside he gives way to the *loathing and bitterness* he feels about his home circumstances.

◑ What details in the opening paragraph suggest that the disorder of the Dedalus household is greater than ever?

Each stage of Stephen's walk across the city rouses associations with some aspect of the new intellectual world that has opened up to him at University College. He has already begun to work out the theory of art explained later in this section. His absorption in his studies has *rapt him from the companionships of youth*, and the other students consider him antisocial.

When not intent on his studies Stephen is *glad to find himself in the midst of common lives, passing on his way amid the squalor and noise and sloth of the city*. The striking of a clock makes him realize he has missed another lecture, and his mind turns to his fellow students. Although the list may seem random, each of them represents some aspect of Stephen's background that he must reject before he can steel himself to abandon Ireland. Look at the character Mind Map on p. 20.

First of all, he imagines himself at the English lecture he is currently missing and sees the bent head of his friend Cranly in front of him. Cranly has a *priestlike face,* and Stephen has confided to him *all the tumults and unrest and longing in his soul.* Another friend, Davin, comes from an uneducated peasant background. He is a fervent supporter of the native Celtic culture and the Catholic Church. Toward both he shows *the attitude of a dullwitted loyal serf.*

Davin has told Stephen about an adventure he had one evening when walking back from a hurling match. He stopped at a cottage to ask for a glass of water. The woman who answered his knock was alone. She invited him to enter the house and spend the night with her, but Davin refused.

Davin's Irish-English is very similar in style to the poetic language of the Irish Revival movement. It is used most notably in the plays of J. M. Synge (*Riders to the Sea, The Playboy of the Western World*). Joyce had a deep contempt for this movement, seeing it as narrowly provincial and backward-looking. His attitude was formed before Ireland was an independent state and the Abbey Theatre acquired its international reputation. (See James Joyce and Ireland, p. 5.)

⊙ What are your reactions to Davin's story? Stephen finds the woman *a type of her race and his own, a batlike soul waking to the consciousness of itself in darkness and secrecy and* *loneliness.* ⊙ What does he mean by this? Where is the phrase used again, and in what context?

While thinking about his friend's adventure, Stephen is stopped by a girl in the street who tries to sell him some flowers. The blue flowers and her young blue eyes seem at first *images of guilelessness* until he sees the reality of *her ragged dress and damp coarse hair and hoydenish face.*

Now Try This

? Bearing in mind that we are not necessarily meant to accept Stephen's view of himself and his situation as reliable, and referring to the later contents of this chapter, how accurate do you consider Stephen's belief that he is *rapt from the companionships of youth*?

? Is Stephen really in touch with *common lives?* What do the words *when this brief pride of silence ... with a light heart* tell us about Stephen?

? Why do you think Joyce puts these two figures of Irish peasant women so close to his description of the wading girl at the end of the last chapter?

Conversation with the dean

Stephen is too late for his French class, so he goes to the physics lecture hall to wait for the next lecture. He finds the dean of studies inside struggling to light a fire, a suitable image for someone who has to "light a fire" in the young minds he supervises. The dean engages Stephen in conversation while continuing his task. Stephen looks down on him, both literally and figuratively.

The dean asks Stephen to define "the beautiful," his mind still half on his efforts to light the fire. He misunderstands first one and then another of Stephen's remarks, and this increases the young man's contempt. Stephen despises the Jesuit priest as a convert to Catholicism and *a poor Englishman in Ireland*. Nevertheless, he feels *a smart of dejection* that the dean is more at home than he with the language of the great English poets. In fact, Stephen is exhibiting the same self-oppression that he dislikes in his fellow countrymen.

Take particular notice of their exchange about the word *tundish*, which is mentioned again and neatly illustrates the above point.

"I shall try to fly by those nets"

Their conversation is interrupted by the entry of the physics class. During the professor's lecture a student named Moynihan tries to catch Stephen's ear with crudely humorous comments. Afterwards, the students stand talking in the entrance hall where MacCann is asking for signatures on a petition associated with the Hague Peace Conference. Cranly reproaches Stephen for being in a bad mood, which he denies. MacCann challenges Stephen over his refusal to sign the petition, and the others join in the dispute.

You will notice the students speaking to each other in snatches of Latin. Until well into this century, nearly all university courses – not just those in ancient languages and literature – required a minimum Latin qualification for admission. This itself was a relic of the Middle Ages, when throughout Europe Latin was the universal language for students and teachers alike. Stephen and his friends are speaking very bad Latin! It should be regarded as a kind of "in" language or slang.

Cranly pulls Stephen away from the group. They are followed by a student named Temple who is anxious to impress Stephen. In the alley another group is playing handball, watched by Davin. He also picks on Stephen and asks why he doesn't support the nationalist Revival movement and the activities that go with it. Davin wishes Stephen hadn't told him about some incidents in his private life, presumably his visits to prostitutes. He urges Stephen *to be one of us. In your heart you are an Irishman.* He also makes a reference to Emma.

Stephen replies with a fierce attack on his countrymen for their treachery toward those who tried to help them reclaim their national identity *from the days of Tone to those of Parnell... When the soul of a man is born in this country there are nets flung at it to hold it back from flight.... I shall try to fly by those nets... Ireland is the old sow that eats her farrow.*

Stephen's attitude toward his native country

? What is the connection between Stephen's conversation with the dean and the paragraph beginning *My ancestors threw off their language ...* ?

? *The old sow that eats her farrow.* Explain.

? What experiences do you think have caused Stephen to feel this way about Ireland?

Take some time off before tackling Stephen's ideas on beauty

What is beauty?

?🦉? After watching the game for a while, Stephen asks Lynch, one of the students, to take a walk with him. While they are doing this he explains his own theory of "aesthetics," that is, an answer to the question, *What is beauty?* (Stephen uses the spelling *esthetics*.) This long, one-sided discussion is interrupted by Lynch's crude sexual jokes, by noises in the street, and by a meeting with another student. Lynch has a short attention span – half the time his mind seems to be on other matters – and Stephen is showing off to a less intelligent companion. The result is a loose argument that goes back and forth and may need some explanation.

THE SOURCES FOR STEPHEN'S THEORY

Stephen bases his theory on statements made by Thomas Aquinas, the great Catholic theologian, and by the ancient Greek philosopher, Aristotle. The combination is not so odd as it seems. Most medieval systems of thought and education were a Christian interpretation of the works of Aristotle.

Like Aristotle in his *Poetics,* Stephen puts forward some general thoughts about beauty, but he is really concerned with literature. Aristotle is concerned with **tragedy**, saying its main aim is to arouse *pity* and *terror* in the audience and so to give an outlet to their emotions. This outlet is known as "catharsis." The same process is at work when some of us cry while watching movies.

> Pity is occasioned by undeserved misfortune, and fear by that of one like ourselves ... the intermediate kind of person, a man not pre-eminently virtuous and just.

The misfortune Aristotle is talking about is not brought on by accident but by an error in judgment. The person who misjudges has some flaw of character that causes him to do this and his character is a mixture of good and bad – like ourselves. Examples of the "flaw" taken from English literature would be King Lear's obstinacy or Macbeth's ambition.

Stephen gives his own definitions of pity and terror. He uses them to insist that *the esthetic emotion* – what Aristotle calls "the tragic pleasure" – is therefore static. *The mind is arrested and raised above desire and loathing.* These two emotions, says Stephen, are *kinetic* and therefore *unesthetic.* They are also *not more than physical.* They are caused by *improper arts,* such as pornography or didacticism. Look up those two terms and also *static* and *kinetic* if you don't know what they mean.

The aesthetic emotion is aroused by *the rhythm of beauty* in a work of art. Different cultures have different standards of beauty; here Stephen indulges the lecherous Lynch by taking female beauty as his example. Underneath the differences, he says, we find the same universal standards. To be truly beautiful a work of art must possess *wholeness, harmony and radiance* – its own special quality. This idea is from Aquinas, but it originated with Aristotle.

Aristotle defines tragedy as the imitation of an action that is "a complete whole, with its several incidents so closely connected that the transposal or withdrawal of any one of them will disjoin and dislocate the whole."

AN EXAMPLE OF WHOLENESS

Stephen points to the basket being carried by a butcher's boy as an example of wholeness. The basket is itself, distinct from everything that surrounds it. He then goes on to harmony ("consonantia"). The object is made up of *the results of its parts and their sum, harmonious. That is consonantia.*

Stephen neglects to mention that the different parts of the work must also be in satisfactory balance with each other if we are to call it "beautiful." Ask someone who knows about the history of furniture to show you a photo of Shaker tables and chairs. They are completely plain and functional because the people who built them disapproved of unnecessary decoration. The result is a style of outstanding beauty that is eagerly sought by modern collectors – quite the opposite of what was intended!

Stephen admits that radiance – claritas – *is rather vague.* He thinks it must refer to the unique, individual nature of an object – *the whatness of a thing.* It is the *supreme quality ... felt by the artist when the esthetic image is first conceived,* that is, it is the artist's moment of inspiration. It is the *enchantment of the heart.*

From Chapter 3 of Aristotle's *Poetics* Stephen takes the idea that there are three forms of art. Like Aristotle he is, of course, referring only to literature. These forms are the lyrical (personal), the epical (narrative), and the dramatic. Aristotle does not place them in order of merit, but Stephen does.

He sees the lyrical as *the simplest verbal gesture of an instant of emotion ... He who utters it is more conscious of the instant of emotion than of himself feeling the emotion.*

"Lyric" poetry is usually a direct expression of the poet's thought or feeling. ❂ Can you think of any examples?

Epical literature emerges out of this simpler form *when ... the centre of emotional gravity is equidistant from the artist himself and from others.* Epic poetry is usually narrative. Examples are Homer's *Iliad* and *Odyssey* and a much later work based on the same form, Milton's *Paradise Lost*.

The dramatic form is reached when ... the personality of the artist ... refines itself out of existence... The artist, like the God of the creation, remains within or behind or beyond or above his handiwork, invisible, refined out of existence, indifferent, paring his finger nails.

During Stephen's discussion with Lynch, rain has begun to fall. When they reach the university library, they find a group of students sheltering under its arcade. Stephen catches sight of Emma among other women students. He still resents what he thinks of as her flirtation with a priest; however, as he listens to the chatter around him, his mood changes, and he wonders if he has judged her too harshly.

Test your understanding of Stephen's theory

?   Looking at *A Portrait* with Stephen's theory in mind, we can say that in its overall movement it progresses through all three forms. Where would you say the *lyrical* form changes to *epical*, and where does the *epical* change to *dramatic*?

?   What are the main points of Stephen's "theory of aesthetics?" See if you can summarize his argument in half a page of separate points. Try to make up a Mind Map for each, or, if you prefer, combine all points into one Mind Map.

award yourself some time off – you deserve it!

SECTION 2

"O *what sweet music*"

Stephen awakes in a mood of rapture – *an enchantment of the heart* – and out of it emerges a villanelle, an intricately rhyming lyric form that depends far more on cleverness than on inspiration.

Stephen's ecstatic awakening is contrasted almost to the point of absurdity with the way he sets about putting his inspiration into words. When he looks for paper and pencil he sees only his encrusted candlestick and *the soup plate he had eaten the rice from for supper.* ❂ What other details of this kind can you pick out? The whole effect is a **caricature** of the starving poet in the attic.

Stephen's villanelle is meant to be about Emma, but the artificial verse pattern draws in religious and romantic imagery that turns it into something much more general. ❂ How does it reflect Stephen's attitude to women?

One of the most ironic aspects of this section is that Stephen produces a poem in "the Celtic twilight" style. This was part of the Revival movement he so much despises, as did Joyce himself. The early poems of W. B. Yeats are good examples of the movement.

After the first three verses Stephen finds his inspiration faltering, so he hastily scribbles them on a torn cigarette package. He broods on his meetings with Emma in her home and at the carnival ball. It is obvious he does not understand her at all and is possibly fantasizing her reactions. Is there a clue to this in the "happy" *air of Greensleeves*?

Stephen is suddenly reminded of the last time he saw Emma. It was in the Irish language class he had left in a fury after seeing her talk to Father Moran. Stephen's jealousy takes the form of associating Emma with other women who have angered or humiliated him. He resents the fact that she will share *her soul's shy nakedness* with a *priested peasant*, rather than with himself, *a priest of eternal imagination*.

This image of himself reawakens Stephen's flow of thought, and he writes two more verses. Will he send them to Emma? No – she might let her family make fun of them. Then Stephen acknowledges that he is being unfair to her. Perhaps, in some mysterious spiritual dimension, she is aware that he loves her. He lets himself give way to a glow of desire in which he is united with *the temptress of his villanelle*.

The relationship between Stephen and Emma

? What do you think of Stephen's attitude toward Emma?
? Why do you think he is unable to tell her about his feelings?
? What is meant by *the house where young men are called by their Christian names a little too soon*?

SECTION 3

Preparing for flight

Stephen stands on the steps of the library watching the swallows dart and flash through the air. He sees himself as an augur – a Roman priest who interpreted the gods' will through the flight of birds. The bird cries shut out *his mother's sobs and reproaches*. Stephen knows that he is moving toward a major decision and acknowledges his fear. The swallows are an omen that he will leave Ireland. They are *birds ever leaving the homes they had built to wander*.

Stephen is seen mixing with his fellow students despite his feelings of superiority. He joins in the rapid leaps between frivolity and serious discussion so typical of undergraduate conversation. Stephen's later discussions with the students may seem to repeat this but if you compare the two passages you will see that Stephen's behavior has radically changed. He has already withdrawn himself from his friends. He keeps silent even when spoken to.

He speaks only twice – once in the library and once when directly challenged by Temple. He has added his companions to the list of those guilty of keeping Ireland shackled to her past.

ASHAMED TO BE IRISH

The swallows have reminded Stephen of some lines in Yeats's verse play, *The Countess Cathleen*. He remembers that the students tried to close it down on the opening night of the Irish National Theatre – later the famous "Abbey."

In the play there is famine in the land. Countess Cathleen sells her soul to two Demon Merchants to buy back the souls of those who have bartered their own for bread. For her charity, Cathleen is forgiven and when she dies is granted a heavenly crown. Look at the remarks of the audience. ✪ Remembering Father Arnall's sermons in Chapter 3, why do you think they objected so strongly? Do you see any similarities between this incident and the treatment of Parnell?

When Stephen leaves the library with Cranly and Dixon they pass *a man of dwarfish stature* who is rumored to be the result of incest in an aristocratic family. Cranly stays behind to speak to him. The encounter raises unpleasant images in Stephen's mind, again connected with the betrayal of Parnell. He has already asked Cranly to speak to him in private but his friend ignores the request until much later.

While they stand with other students on the library steps, Emma walks by. She ignores Stephen and bows to Cranly. Stephen's delight at seeing her is mingled with irritation at Cranly's delay, and nagging doubt about whether Emma has transferred her affections to his friend. He weaves a daydream about her from Elizabethan songs and lyrics and is annoyed

with himself when his thoughts become *secret and enflaming.*
The tickling of a louse crawling over his neck abruptly brings
him back to reality.

At last he manages to persuade Cranly to walk away with him.
During one last moment of delay, Stephen stares angrily at a
hotel associated with the Anglo-Irish masters who rule Ireland.
(See p. 5, James Joyce and Ireland.) This is another chain of
oppression that he needs to break before he can fulfill his
vocation.

What Stephen wants to talk over is a recent quarrel with
his mother. Mrs. Dedalus has asked Stephen to take
Easter Communion, but Stephen has refused. He *will not serve*
– the words of Lucifer. Cranly, a believer, cannot understand
Stephen's agnostic position. Stephen says he neither believes
nor disbelieves in the sacrament of the Eucharist and has no
wish to overcome his doubts.

Cranly tries another approach. He asks Stephen if he loves his
mother. Stephen says he does not understand the question.
Cranly urges him to take Communion even if he doesn't
believe in the doctrine of the Eucharist. It will cost Stephen
nothing, and he would relieve his mother's distress.

Although Mrs. Dedalus's reaction is the very reason why
Stephen has sought Cranly's advice, he does not answer the
point directly. *With assumed carelessness* he cites a number of
eminent figures who detached themselves from their mothers,
leading up to Jesus himself.

DOES STEPHEN BELIEVE IN HIS RELIGION?

The conversation returns to the question of Stephen's belief or
nonbelief in the teachings of his Church. He admits that
behind his refusal to take Communion lies the fear that after all
*the host ... may be the body and blood of the son of God and
not a wafer of bread.*

This is the doctrine of Transubstantiation, one of the main
beliefs dividing Protestants from Roman Catholics and
Orthodox Christians. Stephen has been taught that to make a
sacrilegious Communion in a state of doubt can lead to instant
damnation.

The two young men have walked to a well-off area of Dublin. The villas there give out an *air of wealth and repose,* and the general air of prosperity calms their minds. In the kitchen of one house a servant girl is singing a popular ballad. Her voice reminds Stephen of *the figure of woman as she appears in the liturgy of the church.* Cranly assures him that *sweet Rosie O'Grady* – the subject of the song – is easy to find.

Thoughts and images have been aroused that have a strong pull on Stephen's emotions: the beauty of church liturgy and the attraction of women. Perhaps their present surroundings also prompt the hope that his material circumstances might improve. But the words that spring into Stephen's mind – *Et tu cum Jesu Galilaeo eras* – introduce Peter's denial of Christ. They suggest that Stephen is tempted to betray his ideals.

He decides he must ruthlessly cut himself loose from all these ties if he is to fulfill himself as an artist. Cranly tries to persuade him that his religious doubts are shared by many and need not drive him into exile. Stephen makes an emphatic reply.

I will not serve that in which I no longer believe whether it call itself my home, my fatherland or my church: and I will try to express myself in some mode of life or art as freely as I can ... using the only arms I allow myself to use – silence, exile, and cunning.

Cranly wonders if Stephen realizes the meaning of the word *alone.* Indirectly he offers him undying friendship. Stephen concludes that the offer is a reflection of Cranly's *cold sadness ... his own loneliness which he feared.*

Think about Stephen's family situation

?   Should Stephen have done what his mother wanted?

stop here before tackling the final section of the book

SECTION 4

Stephen's diary

The last section in the novel consists of Stephen's diary entries for the five weeks from March 20 to April 27. This is the "dramatic" mode of writing referred to earlier in the book. The character, Stephen, is presented to us directly without the presence of the artist, Joyce.

These entries consist of a mixture of events, thoughts, and dreams. Most of them are casually jotted down in a style that complements and balances the opening section of the novel. There are also more carefully written passages. Between them, the entries sum up the problems that have confronted Stephen as he has grown from infancy to young manhood.

STEPHEN'S OPINION OF CRANLY

The first entry records Stephen's conversation with Cranly. He writes that he has been *supple and suave.* ❷ What does this mean? Do you agree with him?

Stephen thinks about the possibility that Cranly is the child of elderly parents. This leads to the comparison with John the Baptist, the *precursor* of Christ. ❷ Look back and find other imagery suggesting this. By implication, Stephen himself is Christ.

His absurd egotism – many would consider it blasphemy – reminds us that we must see Stephen in double focus. The mind and talent of an artist are struggling to break out of the chrysalis of a conceited, immature, young man. His efforts to reach the detachment he thinks necessary to the artist – *invisible, ... indifferent, paring his finger nails* are expressed in behavior that is the consequence of his conceit and immaturity. See p. 30 for a fuller discussion of this point.

There are several entries about Emma. Stephen has not seen her for some time and is afraid she may be ill (24 March). He has a glimpse of her in a city tea shop (2 April), and wonders again if Cranly is seeking her favor behind his back. They have a last encounter on 15 April when they meet by accident on Grafton Street.

After she has wished him good luck and said good-bye, Stephen manages to take a more objective view of their relationship. *I liked her and it seems a new feeling to me.*

STYLE AND LANGUAGE

The images of travel become more emphatic as the entries near their end. On 10 April *the sound of hoofs* is worked up into a prose poem on Stephen's imminent departure. There is another on 16 April. In Stephen's mind *the white arms of roads ... and the black arms of tall ships* have replaced the embraces he had hoped for from Emma. He is now ready to set out and *to forge in the smithy of my soul the uncreated conscience of my race.*

The novel ends with a final invocation to Daedalus, the *old artificer* whom Stephen now claims as his true father.

Test yourself

? See if you can pick up other themes from this section. What is Stephen's final attitude to his mother (24 March, 30 March) *still harping on the mother* (26 April)?

? What does he have to say about Irish culture (24 March, 14 April)? In what way is Stephen afraid of the old man?

? How does Stephen interpret the image of the crocodile? After the puzzle story, it is mentioned three times.

? Why is Stephen so angry to find that *tundish* is *good old blunt English*? What is the link between this and his reaction to the discussion with Father Charles Ghezzi: *Then went to college ... the overcoat of the crucified*?

congratulate yourself – you have made it to the end of the novel!

TOPICS FOR DISCUSSION AND BRAINSTORMING

One of the best ways to review is with one or more friends. Even if you're with someone who hardly knows the text you are studying, you'll find that having to explain things to your friend will help you to organize your own thoughts and memorize key points.

Discussion will also help you to develop interesting new ideas that perhaps neither of you would have had alone. Use a brainstorming approach to tackle any of the topics listed below. Allow yourself to share whatever ideas come into your head – however meaningless they seem. They will get you thinking creatively.

Use Mind Mapping (see p. v) to help you brainstorm and organize your ideas.

Any of the topics below could appear on an exam, but even if you think you've found one on your actual exam, be sure to answer the precise question given.

TOPICS

1 Why, at the end of *A Portrait*, does Stephen feel that he has to leave Ireland?

2 Do you find Stephen a sympathetic or unsympathetic hero? Give reasons for your answer.

3 What did you find original or different about *A Portrait* compared with other novels you have read that describe childhood and adolescence?

4 Choose **two** of the following and write a brief character sketch of each. What influence do they have on Stephen?
Mr. Dedalus; Dante; the dean of studies; Cranly; Davin.

5 Discuss Joyce's use of imagery in *A Portrait*.

6 Discuss Stephen's relationships with young girls and women of all ages as he grows up.

7 Briefly relate the story of Icarus and his father Daedzlus; then show how Joyce used the myth as the foundation of his novel.

8 What effect did Stephen's harsh, intimidating experiences at school have on his personality?

HOW TO GET AN "A" IN ENGLISH LITERATURE

In all your study, in coursework, and in exams, be aware of the following:

- **Characterization** – the characters and how we know about them (what they say and do, how the author describes them), their relationships, and how they develop.
- **Plot and structure** – what happens and how the plot is organized into parts or episodes.
- **Setting and atmosphere** – the changing scene and how it reflects the story (for example, a storm reflecting a character's emotional difficulties).
- **Style and language** – the author's choice of words, and literary devices such as imagery, and how these reflect the mood.
- **Viewpoint** – how the story is told (for example, through an imaginary narrator, or in the third person but through the eyes of one character – "She was furious – how dare he!").
- **Social and historical context** – influences on the author (see Background in this guide).

Develop your ability to:

- Relate **detail** to **broader content, meaning, and style**.
- Show understanding of the author's **intentions, technique, and meaning** (brief and appropriate comparisons with other works by the same author will earn credit).
- Give **personal response and interpretation**, backed up by **examples** and short **quotations**.
- **Evaluate** the author's achievement (how far does the author succeed and why?).

Make sure you:

- Know how to use paragraphs correctly.
- Use a wide range of **vocabulary** and sentence structure.
- Use **short**, appropriate quotations as **evidence** of your understanding of that part of the text.
- Use **literary terms** to show your understanding of what the author is trying to achieve with language.

THE EXAM ESSAY

Planning

A literary essay of about 250 to 400 words on a theme from *A Portrait of the Artist* will challenge your skills as an essay writer. It is worth taking some time to plan your essay carefully. An excellent way to do this is in the three stages below:

1 Make a **Mind Map of** your ideas on the theme suggested. Brainstorm and write down any ideas that pop into your head.
2 Taking ideas from your Mind Map, **organize** them into an outline choosing a logical sequence of information. Choose significant details and quotations to support your main thesis.
3 Be sure you have both a strong **opening paragraph** stating your main idea and giving the title and author of the literary work you will be discussing, and a **conclusion** that sums up your main points.

Writing and Editing

Write your essay carefully, allowing at least five minutes at the end to check for errors of fact as well as for correct spelling, grammar, and punctuation.

REMEMBER!

Stick to the thesis you are trying to support and avoid unneccessary plot summary. Always support your ideas with relevant details and quotations from the text.

Model Answer and Plan

The next (and final) chapter consists of a model essay on a theme from *A Portrait of the Artist* followed by a Mind Map and an essay plan used to write it. Use these to get an idea of how an essay about *A Portrait of the Artist* might be organized and how to break up your information into a logical sequence of paragraphs.

Before reading the answer, you might like to do a plan of your own, then compare it with the example. The numbered points with comments at the end show why it's a good answer.

MODEL ANSWER AND ESSAY PLAN

QUESTION

How is the theme of "martyrdom" used in *A Portrait*?

PLAN SUMMARY
1 Define "martyr."
2 Stephen – sensitive – suffers.
3 Examples: Eileen, cesspool, pandied. "Chooses"?
4 Instinct to reason – imagery underlines connection.
5 Artist must be true to self.
6 Belvedere – thinks for self.
7 University – a) speaks out, b) Identifies with Tone and Parnell.
8 Theme also used to support narrative structure.

ESSAY

Joyce's hero is named after St. Stephen, who was the first Christian martyr. A martyr is someone who suffers for a belief that he or she refuses to give up. This provides us with a clue to the writer's intention.[1]

In a general sense Stephen is martyred from his earliest days. He has a sensitive nature that clashes with the values of the society into which he is born long before he decides to reject them. Yet, can we really say that he "chooses" to suffer?

As a very young child, Stephen says he will marry his friend, Eileen Vance. For this he is threatened with horrific punishment by his nurse, Dante. She tries to end their friendship because Eileen is a Protestant and the Dedalus family is Catholic. Stephen doesn't realize that he is rebelling against his religion.

He is bullied when he goes to his first school, Clongowes Wood College. He is sensitive and imaginative and not interested in sports, perhaps because he is handicapped by poor eyesight. All this sets him apart from the other students.

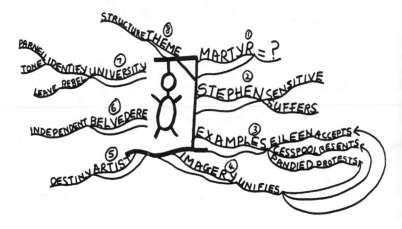

He is pushed into the cesspool by a classmate who relies on the one thing Stephen does share with them: the schoolboy code of not "ratting." Cold and wet from his dunking, he becomes seriously ill.

Later Stephen is unfairly "pandied" by Father Dolan, who refuses to believe that he has broken his glasses. Stephen is so outraged that despite his fear he goes to complain to the rector, who promises to set things right. Stephen's real martyrdom comes after he has left Clongowes and discovers that the two priests laughed at the fuss he made.[2]

In these three incidents we see Stephen changing from a child acting on instinct into someone who knows the reason for his decisions. Throughout the book Joyce uses imagery and symbolism to point out the close connection between Stephen's actions from infancy to adulthood. Everything that finally makes him cut himself off from his background can be seen in miniature in the first section of the book.

So, even when Stephen is a young child we cannot divide his sufferings into "chosen" and "unchosen" and say that only some of them are those of a "martyr." Joyce seems to be saying that a genuine artist cannot help being true to himself, whatever the cost, even when he is too young to be aware of his destiny.[3]

The theme of martyrdom appears more openly in later sections of the book. For instance, at Belvedere, his second school, Stephen is accused of heresy by one of his teachers. He is physically attacked by his new classmates for asserting that Byron is a better poet than Tennyson. We see that he is punished because he insists on thinking for himself.

These and other incidents arise when Stephen reacts against the pressures to conform that are put upon him by others. However, when he goes to the university, the theme broadens in two ways. Until then he has kept his opinions to himself. Now he stands up for them in public and argues with his friends. A good example is when Stephen refuses to sign MacCann's petition for world peace.[4]

Secondly, Stephen's own personal history is compared with that of others, and this gives the theme much more force and depth. The betrayal of Parnell gave rise to the quarrel at the Dedalus Christmas dinner. There Joyce used it to show how adult bickering damaged Stephen's sense of security. Now the betrayal is quoted to highlight the treachery of the Irish toward those who try to help them. Stephen says to the other students, "Ireland is the old sow that eats her farrow."

By implication he is including himself with Tone and Parnell, and this, in turn, justifies Stephen's decision to leave Ireland in order to escape their fate.[5]

To sum up, the theme of martyrdom is used in several different ways in *A Portrait*. Like the other themes it appears from beginning to end. So, besides helping us to understand Joyce's ideas, it also reinforces the narrative structure.[6]

WHAT'S SO GOOD ABOUT IT?

1 This defines the question and shows the direction the essay will take.
2 Three relevant examples that illustrate the point. They are summarized briefly with just enough detail to demonstrate that the candidate recalls them accurately.
3 The examples are used to reach a conclusion. This shows that the candidate has a personal opinion about the book, a plus point, even if the examiner does not agree.
4 The essay topic is developed from another angle.
5 ... and developed further.
6 The conclusion rounds off the essay by summing up and adding a final point.

GLOSSARY OF LITERARY TERMS

context   the social and historical influences on the author.

caricature   describing a character's behavior in an exaggerated and humorous way, but not beyond the point of recognition.

epiphany   a festival in the Christian calendar, but used by Joyce to describe some moment of intense emotional revelation.

hagiography   the writing or the study of the lives of Christian saints.

irony   ridiculing an opinion or belief by pretending to hold it, or pretending to be ignorant of the true facts.

lyric verse   short poems that directly express the poet's own thoughts and emotions.

parody   a passage of prose or verse that imitates a particular author's style, usually for comic effect.

prose poetry   vivid prose characterized by the kind of imagery and language usually found in poetry. Not to be confused with overwritten flowery passages!

Revival   specifically used in *A Portrait* about Ireland, but applied to the culture of any nation where its native traditions find renewed life.

satire   writing that makes fun of its subject, often through exaggeration or mock seriousness.

stream of consciousness   an attempt by writers from the late nineteenth century on to give a complete description of the thoughts and feelings flowing through the minds of their fictional characters.

structure   how the plot is organized.

symbolism   the use of objects or even abstract qualities to signify something associated with them. *A Portrait* is particularly rich in its use of symbols, such as the red and green colors of Dante's hairbrushes.

tragedy   a play in which some flaw in the chief character brings on a series of misfortunes ending in a final catastrophe that resolves the situation.

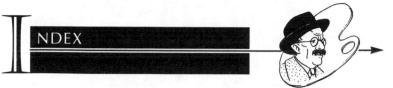